Marbles, Marella Jubes and Milk Bottles

My Golden Years of Australian Childhood

Marbles, Marella Jubes and Milk Bottles

My Golden Years of Australian Childhood

By
SIMON KING

CONSCIOUS CARE PUBLISHING PTY LTD

MARBLES, MARELLA JUBES AND MILK BOTTLES
My Golden Years of Australian Childhood

First Published 2017 by: Conscious Care Publishing Pty Ltd
PO Box 776, Rockingham, WA 6968, Australia
Phone: (61+) 1300 814 115 www.consciouscarepublishing.com

First Edition printed November 2017.

National Library of Australia Cataloguing-in-Publication entry:
Author: King, Simon 1950-
Marbles, Marella Jubes and Milk Bottles / by Simon King
ISBN 780648085447 (Paperback)
Philippa Freegard, Editor.

Printed by Lightning Source
Typeset & cover design by Conscious Care Publishing Pty Ltd

B/KIN

ISBN: 978-0-6480854-4-7

Dedication

This book is dedicated to my parents for their pioneering courage and dogged resilience in commencing a new life with a very young family and limited financial resources on undeveloped land in semi-rural Victoria, Australia, in the early 1950s. Their mutual dedication in establishing a wonderful home occupied for almost fifty years was exemplified by personal hardships endured in successfully raising three children to adulthood, while instilling in them respect for the values of decency, honesty and hard work. Such an enjoyable upbringing has inspired me to finally recognise their devoted efforts in this book.

Acknowledgements

The process of retracing the considerable diverse and often unusual experiences of my childhood has been greatly assisted by the thorough and comprehensive compilation of the residential history of my local home district by the late author Dot Morrison in her unique 2008 publication *Langwarrin: Settlers and Soldiers*. Ms Morrison's research was based substantially on interviews with many local pioneering families — an approach which, to my knowledge, had never been done before in Langwarrin. Many of my own salient recollections were refreshed by her account.

It is also important to acknowledge the contribution of the Mornington Peninsula Family History Society and the Frankston City Library for their invaluable assistance in my narrative journey. I endeavour here to reproduce and share some very special times that are long since gone but never forgotten.

Preface

For any child who lived through the 1950s and early 1960s in Australia, it was an extraordinary time. My life was no different. I was the youngest in a small family intent on starting a new life in a semi-rural area of the country, commencing with scant financial resources, but with a distinctive pioneering spirit to succeed in endeavours through hard work and sheer determination. Living standards in the nation were slowly undergoing transformation following the end of the Second World War, and families were increasingly optimistic about the future. It was a time for our country to prosper after so many years of economic constraint and material shortages.

In many ways, my childhood experiences mirrored this new emerging golden era of popular optimism and immense growth about to envelop a country previously restricted by the ravages of the war. Starting in the early 1950s, my book traces the wonderful family and community freedoms experienced by youngsters adapting to a rural life, and explores the many challenges, choices and delights associated with those times. It provides insight into daily domestic life, personal hobbies, community attractions and celebrations, family travels and a primary education system provided to meet the needs of the burgeoning population. Those were uniquely enjoyable and far simpler times than the present modern era.

My perspective of the latter years of the 50s follows the innumerable innovations and changes that progressively dawned in our society as the past was swept away by the introduction of many modern affordable conveniences, particularly television that made the world seem so much smaller. By the early 60s, this era was still underway and yet many of my childhood interests previously taken for granted were also vanishing as a new booming Australia emerged, and secondary schooling beckoned.

The narrative intentionally quotes most of the physical elements of currency, distances, areas, weights and other similar measures in the Imperial system of measurement prevailing for that era, and designates the equivalent metric system values of today more for sensible comparison purposes. This is to provide the reader with a realistic sense of the golden era of the 1950s and early 1960s.

My purpose for writing this book has been twofold, including providing the reader with a snapshot of a wonderful bygone youth in the context of personal freedoms, adventures and mishaps, and other great stories from a time when a child's pocket money could stretch a very long way. It has also afforded me the luxury of savouring these experiences all over again, so I guess it has worked both ways. Enjoy the uncomplicated wonderful times of this era and all that it provided.

Contents

List of Figures

The Changing Face of Australia

The 1950s was a socially conservative decade in Australia and yet children of that era were offered greater opportunities than any previous or following generation. The nation's birth rate soared as many returned from the Second World War to start new families, necessitating enormous growth in homes and infrastructure to cope. It required a sustainable industrial boom to establish a radically new Australia than that before the war, with superior living standards and affordable conveniences such as home ownership, a new car and a longer, better period of education for children.[1]

Families became substantially smaller than in previous decades with an average of only three children, but overseas immigration predominantly from Europe exceeded a staggering one million new citizens to support the impetus for change.[2] It was the Australian dream to herald a new era of progress and optimism, providing mass production and consumption to satisfy everyone's needs. Australians had always largely considered themselves as British subjects, with education and parliamentary systems based upon around those of Britain. Now it was time for the nation to develop in a new direction, and this would be assisted by the introduction of many previously unimaginable changes – motor cars transformed cities by providing new mobility, aeroplanes connected the nation to other countries, mechanised farming improvements yielded bulk harvesting bonanzas, whilst factories resumed production and provided new and affordable products and time-saving appliances.[3]

It was a simpler time with personal entertainment still initially provided by radios and motion picture theatres. Higher rates of car ownership led to the introduction of drive-in theatres in 1954, and television only arrived in 1956. Automobiles soon dominated road transport, parking meters appeared across many cities and large towns for the first time, and interstate coach travel grew to support an increasing volume of holiday makers keen to see the country. Many Australians going overseas opted for travel by ship due to the enormous cost of air travel. So much was changing, such as the original corner grocery store and the larger variety shops slowly being replaced by the American concept of self-service supermarkets, albeit on a modest scale. Shopping precincts appeared in new suburbs that emerged around capital cities, but home deliveries such as bread, milk and block ice for domestic refrigeration purposes remained popular.[4]

Other fundamental essentials remained largely unchanged. These included a reliance upon public telephone boxes, mailed letters, and telegrams for routine and urgent communications, café dining with limited cuisine choices, prolific bookshops and newsagents for reading matter, families taking their holidays at the seaside, and the crucial 6 pm closing time at hotel bars in Victoria until the mid-1960s. Schooling through the 50s was largely regimented and focused on providing mandatory learning skills essential for later adult life. It could be harsh, with severe punishment for errant pupils by caning or perhaps a whack across the knuckles.[5] By the end of the decade, the face of Australia was barely recognisable as material change transformed most aspects of the nation's way of life, and it was to be irreversible.

I was fortunate to be born in 1950, and consequently spent my entire childhood raised in a country undergoing this new golden era. Australia was still recuperating from the many ravages and domestic upheavals of the Second World War when the 50s dawned. It was a nation that had to be rebuilt with scarce material resources severely depleted by the war effort, and a labour force severely reduced by wartime casualties and broken families. The challenges that lay ahead would ultimately require many years of struggle and uncertainty for some people, yet prosperity and a vastly improved quality of living for others. It would be the start of an entirely new era of opportunity for the nation, founded upon creating a superior standard of living and education for all.

The basis for this national revival was a massive ongoing program of urban construction to meet the needs of new immigrants flooding into the country and Australians returning from the war keen to establish families ('the Baby Boom'). It would include the creation of new suburbs, the refashioning of old, dilapidated inner-city suburbs, and the provision of essential infrastructure to support such a rapidly growing population. This era eventually generated unprecedented growth, rising incomes and the introduction of modern solutions to address the backlog of development required.

At the forefront of this generational change were Australia's children who would eventually become our future citizens, and thus the prerequisite to provide them with social stability through improved education and an adequate home foundation. The education system would foster learning and instil discipline, but it would be the home environment that would nurture the youth of Australia after such a traumatic period of world history. A suitably succinct definition of the term 'home' by Seamus Patrick O'Hanlon is provided: 'A house is a physical structure built to shelter humans. Home is what a house becomes when its inhabitants invest the dwelling with meaning.'[6]

Robert Menzies, the longest-serving Prime Minister in our country's history (1949-1966), offered the following definition:

> One of the best instincts in us is that which induces us to have one little piece of earth with a house and a garden which is ours, to which we can withdraw, in which we can be among friends, into which no stranger can come against our will.[7]

Of course to a child in the early 50s, a home was far more than simply a cosy place to share with your parents, or a secure sanctuary to which to retreat once it got dark outside. A home and its surrounding neighbourhood represented many sources of interest from a child's perspective; play areas and open spaces including natural reserves and nearby parks, creeks, vacant land and anywhere else exciting requiring exploration or discovery, communal out-of-bounds areas where one was forbidden by parents to go, and friends' homes. To have the personal freedom to enjoy these places, a child needed enough space, and ideally, the independence even at a very young age to make these decisions.[8]

The following quotation by children's folklorist Dr Dorothy Howard who studied the specific folklore of Australian children throughout the country in 1954-5 addresses such a dilemma:

> … children played on open paddocks, earthy playgrounds and sandy footpaths, and could dig their marble holes anywhere they chose. In the 1950s, with the population concentrated more and more in city areas, with more hard-surfaced playgrounds and footpaths, the old hole marble games seemed to be diminishing in favor of surface games played on diagrams of various shapes.[9]

Although being raised on the rural fringe of suburbia, and so able to enjoy the benefits of a semi-rural life, I still experienced the personal hardships involved in commencing a new family life with only limited financial resources.

My Childhood Stamping Ground

The story of where I spent the golden era of my early childhood in Australia is intrinsically interlinked between the popular bayside outer Melbourne suburb of Frankston, and the nearby semi-rural district of Langwarrin in the State of Victoria (originally named 'the Port Phillip District'). Both locations have particularly intriguing histories of early settlement.

Frankston is situated at the northern extremity of the Mornington Peninsula on the eastern shoreline of Port Phillip Bay.

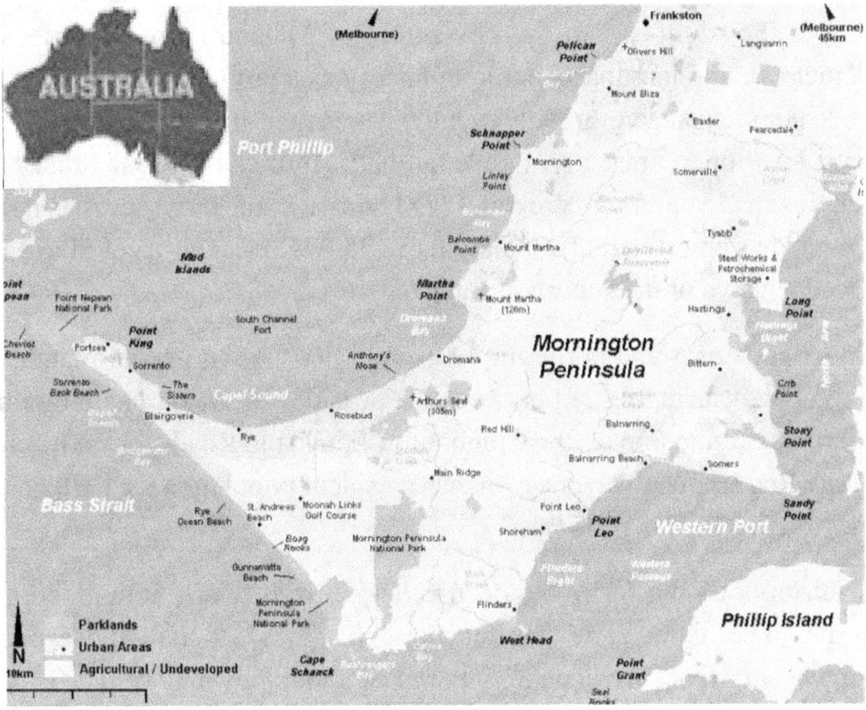

Figure 1: A Basic Map of Mornington Peninsula
(©Nick Carson, English Wikipedia: original
inset with Australia map)

European settlement of Frankston began with a small unofficial fishing village following the foundation of Melbourne on 30 August 1835.[1] Fishermen were among the earliest Europeans to settle the area, living in tents and wattle and daub huts/shacks on or near its foreshore, and travelling by boat to the early Melbourne settlement to sell their catches. It remained isolated from Melbourne and only reached by a rough track or by sea.[2,3]

From the following account, it appears that living conditions even in Melbourne were relatively rudimentary in those times:

> ...Melbourne was no more than an unnamed little shanty town, – if that. Early in 1836, visitors described it as consisting of about a dozen wattle and daub or turf huts, and the same number of tents ... a six-roomed hotel of a very primitive order ... with nothing to eat nor a place to sleep in.[4]

Frankston was officially established as a village in 1854.[5] Due to its proximity to the south-east of the city centre of Melbourne of 26 miles (41 kilometres), and its subsequent long history as a prominent seaside resort, Frankston's expansive growth eventually resulted in it being proclaimed a city by 1966.[6] Presently, Frankston City (formerly City of Frankston) occupies an area of 51 square miles (131 square kilometres) across ten suburbs and has an estimated population of 135,971 residents as of 30th June, 2015, inclusive of the suburb of Langwarrin.[7]

Further eastwards and bordering Frankston lies the semi-rural inland suburb of Langwarrin, nestled between the seaside resort and next adjoining suburb of Cranbourne on the Cranbourne-Frankston Road (formerly Cranbourne Road). Langwarrin's estimated resident population as at 30th June 2015 totalled 23,635 residents.[8]

The history of Langwarrin has been rather convoluted and at times confusing due to so many name and boundary changes, so I shall endeavour to keep the narrative succinct and only relevant to my own story. The earliest white settlement of the district was by squatters. The name Langwarrin comes from the squatting run called either *Lang Waring* or *Long Waring*, leased by William Willoby from 1843. It took a long time for Willoby to obtain his run, and hence the name *Longwaring* comes from "long waiting".[9]

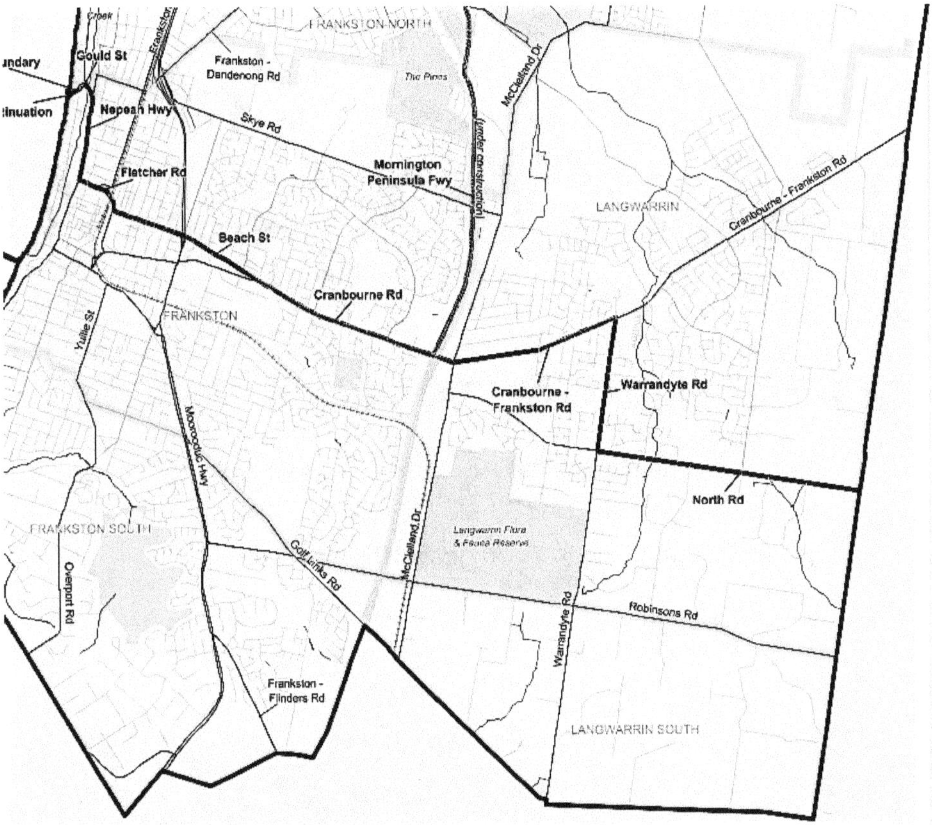

Figure 2: Langwarrin District (Frankston City Council Map LEGL./11-115, © Victorian Electoral Commission, State Government of Victoria, 2011: cropped original with no ward labels)

The early pioneers and shrewd land investors of the 1800s held substantial tracts of 'old Langwarrin', but it was probably towards the late 1800s when development really commenced. By the 1880s, Langwarrin was occupied by corn farmers and orchardists, and a village known as *Langwarren Estate* was surveyed as a town in 1886, built around a saw mill which employed many locals.[10]

Figure 3: Langwarrin Estate View looking North West ca.1880-ca.1890 (Troedel & Co. Lithographer, State Library of Victoria Image H2000. 180/291a)

Figure 4: Langwarrin Estate View looking South East from Mt.Grandview ca.1880-ca.1890 (Troedel & Co. Lithographer, State Library of Victoria Image H2000. 180/291a)

This was also the time when ongoing encampments of Colonial defence troops began at the newly established Langwarrin Military Reserve that was situated at a strategic elevated location to defend Melbourne and Port Phillip Bay from potential sea attack.[11] It was a prudent decision in the event of any likely invading force instead using Western Port Bay located further south of Langwarrin to disembark, as troops and supplies could be quickly mobilised from the Reserve.

The demise of the 'old Langwarrin' followed the end of a 3-year land boom in the district which finished in 1893 and resulted in a 'new Langwarrin' springing up, based on Warrandyte Road and close to the Military Reserve of 549 acres (222 hectares).[12] Prior to the First World War, this reserve was used over several years mainly for temporary encampments of volunteer soldiery from throughout Victoria held at Easter or after New Year, and at the outbreak of war, as a detention centre for enemy aliens, particularly Germans.[13]

This extensive tract of land at the south eastern end of Langwarrin still covers 214 hectares today and represents a significant place in military history between 1886 and 1979. It subsequently became the Langwarrin Flora and Fauna Reserve – one of the few remaining areas on the south eastern fringe of Melbourne for such conservation of indigenous flora and fauna, representing 45 per cent of all flora species native to the Mornington Peninsula.[14]

In 1900, Langwarrin was a rural village with the people clearing their land for dairying, orchards and stock. Despite having little money, they owned land and were able to grow their own fruit and vegetables and have some poultry. Importantly, with no building restrictions, most built their own houses. This community remained small and unchanged through the Depression and the Second World War until servicemen eventually returned to the district, married and commenced building additional homes. Electricity was finally connected to the district in 1947.[15]

Figure 5: First Electric Light Pole being erected in Cranbourne Road, Frankston, c.1919 (Frankston City Libraries, Frankston Local History Album LHV11, p.28)

Langwarrin was always considered to be more bush than town, and a widespread country community rather than a township, as it did not have a concentration of the stores and facilities usually found in most rural townships. In the 1950s, there were three separate general stores spread along the western end of Cranbourne Road; *Arcadia* operated as a hardware shop and post office with a single petrol bowser, and the two others as petrol station/garages selling convenience merchandise. One of these garages was located on the intersection of Warrandyte Road with Cranbourne Road. There was also a far older fourth general store located at the furthermost end of Warrandyte Road, but I rarely ventured that far from my home.

At the eastern end of Cranbourne Road closer to Cranbourne, yet another general store with a petrol pump was eventually established in 1959 at the relatively small community area of Centreville. It was advertised as '…a General Store, Milk Bar, Service Station, and Authorised Newsagent with

Kodak supplies'.[16]

Whilst I resided in Langwarrin, it was historically an integral part of the rural Shire of Cranbourne (latterly City of Cranbourne) until December 1994 when the encroaching urban sprawl of substantial residential development resulted in the suburb's integration with the City of Frankston, as part of a statewide reform of local government.[17] In some respects, this history of rural beginnings associated with the Shire of Cranbourne indicates why the area developed in such a way, with a community of predominantly small landholdings of poultry farmers, orchardists, and dairy producers, as well as a smattering of sand pits spread throughout the district.

Langwarrin had no distinctive township in the 1950s, and in 1954 had a very small population of only 577 residents, according to the Commonwealth of Australia's Census.[18] By the next census in 1961, the population, although growing, was still only 844 in comparison with nearby Frankston's population of 26,722.[19] Langwarrin thus remained a relatively small semi-rural community on the fringe of suburbia.

Every community possibly has at least one famous resident, and Langwarrin was privileged to have been home for two public figures. The late Dame Elisabeth Murdoch, AC (Order of Australia), DBE (Dame Commander of the Order of the British Empire), philanthropist and mother of international media magnate Rupert Murdoch, frequently resided at various times on the vast estate of *Cruden Farm*, opposite our home on Cranbourne Road. The property, since extended, covers 135 acres (54.6 hectares) and was purchased as a wedding present when she married in 1928. Dame Elisabeth's magnificent gardens at *Cruden Farm* and nearby extensive Arboretum remain a delightful horticultural experience for the public.

Figure 6: Cruden Farm Estate ca.1920-ca.1948
(Photographer: Ruth Hollick, State Library of
Victoria Image H2004. 61/500)

The famous author Nevil Shute Norway wrote his best-selling novel *On the Beach* in 1956 under his pen name of Nevil Shute whilst at his magnificent hilltop property on farmland at Robinson's Road in Langwarrin South. It became a feature film of the same title in 1959 adapted from the book, concerning the tragic aftermath of a nuclear war on a mixed group of survivors in Melbourne, and was one of the first major Hollywood movies to be made in Australia, partially filmed in Frankston.[20]

Settling in Langwarrin

In 1952 not quite two years after my birth, the family moved from New South Wales in a small caravan towed by our open-topped late 1920s Chrysler tourer to the semi-rural district of Langwarrin. My parents had purchased a substantial one acre (0.4 hectare) block of undeveloped land for a very modest fee on Cranbourne Road which was the only thoroughfare to Frankston. With few neighbours and no public facilities available other than electricity, it was a daunting challenge. It was to be a fresh start for a young family with three children from interstate in an untouched pristine environment somewhere in the bush.

Figure 7: Early days

The uncleared block was adjacent to a large nature reserve (eventually established in 1985-86 as an Arboretum) on one side and a young family of Dutch immigrants on the other. Cruden Farm occupied the opposite side of Cranbourne Road from our home over an extensive distance. The block had a quiet country setting and was almost indistinguishable from the adjacent thickly wooded nature reserve, yet was barely three miles (five kilometres) from Port Phillip Bay on the coast. To understand the pioneering hardships that we eventually experienced, you need to appreciate true isolation and how we adapted to suit these circumstances. For the first few years, we were not connected to the mains power supply on Cranbourne Road due to our limited finances, and relied instead upon kerosene-fuelled 'hurricane' lanterns for night lighting.

Such lanterns were flat-wicked portable lamps made of soldered, tin-plated sheet steel stampings with a swivel wire handle and a flat base. They were most effectively either hung outside or positioned indoors seated on a flat surface. The resultant burning odours and potential risk of fire from tipping over eventually resulted in their replacement with the safer wick mantle lamps that produced far brighter light for reading purposes. Prior to the period of affordable cold storage refrigerators and with no financial access to electric power, we had to keep perishable food from deteriorating by innovative solutions. There were only three possible options: delivery of large solid blocks of ice to maintain a cool temperature for such foods in a non-mechanical icebox, consume perishable foods without undue delay, or install the famous 'Coolgardie safe'.

Block ice deliveries in those bygone days did not extend to our semi-rural property and for a family of five, it was impractical to store perishables beyond one or two days in the warmer months. The Coolgardie safe comprised a wooden-framed shelved cabinet with a latched door enclosed entirely by fly-proof fine wire mesh, with a galvanised iron tray on top filled with water, and the cabinet shrouded in hessian with one end soaking in the tray of water to gradually saturate the entire fabric. By clever placement of this cabinet to catch any passing breeze, the water-saturated hessian shrouding would slowly evaporate its contained moisture, in turn cooling the contents of the safe. For an invention dating back to the late

1890s, it certainly stood the test of time for prolonging the quality of meats and fresh produce.[1] Eventually as the children grew much older, we opted for a kerosene-fuelled refrigerator as the next best alternative, given our extreme summers. This temperamental and noisy unit was satisfactory until we finally installed an electrical version once connected to the power grid in later years.

Drinking water was produced from rainwater saved in a large corrugated and galvanised mild steel tank, and hot water generated for washing and ablutions through a wood-burner fuelled with fallen conifer (pine) cones and dead eucalyptus tree branches. Personal heating in winter was achieved by adding an extra blanket on one's bed at night or wearing more woollen pullovers in the daytime. Our water storage tank only had one major drawback over the years, and that was the need to prevent local pesky tree possums from using it as a swimming chamber.

For clothes washing, the process was certainly convoluted. All soiled garments were boiled for hours in a massive copper pot heated by a wood fire underneath, removed and drained manually, and then vigorously rubbed on a ribbed scrubbing board/washboard. The wet clothes were then soaked in fresh rainwater poured into twin concrete rinse tubs, and all excess water removed by either arduously squeezing the wet items by hand or compressing them through a hand-cranked roller clothes-wringer.

Clothing and bed linen were dried naturally in the sunlight by hanging them on a wire line tautly strung between two trees and propped-up with a forked stick in the middle of the line to keep items from touching the ground. The washing smelled as fresh and looked almost as new as when first purchased. Interestingly, the twin concrete tubs were also ideal for bathing the younger children until a porcelain bath tub could be purchased.

Our first priority beyond establishing living essentials was to build a house suitable for a family of five, and that ultimately would take a considerable period of years. As a result, two bungalows were initially constructed nearby for 'temporary' accommodation and the original caravan put to further good use for storage purposes. All three structures would remain in active use for several years and a permanent feature of our property due to the prolonged period taken to build our house.

Figure 8: Twin Bungalows (The Pink Room in background and Fibro-Cement Room in foreground)

The first bungalow built was an all-timber, single-room large cabin, with double bunks at one end for sleeping two adults and two small children, and a compact living area at the other end with comfortable chairs, a massive cathedral-style radio and gramophone for entertainment, a table and various shelves. This was to be our living quarters for years to come. Its exterior was painted in garish pink to preserve the wood from weathering and promptly came to be named 'the Pink Room'; an apt title that remained with the bungalow forever. The roof was made of thin overlapping sheets of corrugated tin, with no interior insulation to reduce heat or preclude leakage from rainfall, but still reasonably sealed. In winter, the thunderous roar of rain on this roof could be deafening at times, whilst in summer, it was often excessively hot inside the bungalow.

The second timber bungalow was a more modest smaller building, with only fibro-cement sheeting for the exterior and another corrugated tin roof. This dwelling was to house my older brother who was into his early teenage years, and was designed as a bedroom and study. Once construction of the family house was eventually underway, a working kitchen for meal preparation and dining was first on the agenda, followed by a suitable bathroom. Our local outdoor latrine, also known as the outhouse, dunny, privy (archaic variant of 'private') or 'little house', had been installed as the home's toilet not long after we arrived on the property, and it fulfilled its purpose for many years before a mains sewage system was installed.

It was sensibly located at the undeveloped rear corner of the property fur-

Figure 9: The little house

thermost from our dwellings, with a twisting path of small stepping pavers thoughtfully laid to track its location in the dark. On any night of heavy rainfall, the stepping pavers remained just above the streamlets of water that flooded our property and thus greatly assisted me in reaching 'the dunny' without receiving wet soaking feet. During winter nights, a hurricane lantern was carried to safely negotiate that path and to light the interior of the outhouse.

Unfortunately, on hot summer evenings, this lantern only served to attract swarms of mosquitoes and other bugs inside the outhouse, so it was smarter to rely upon developing your night vision instead. There were always frequent fears that spiders might inhabit the latrine's seat, and most particularly at night. Consequently, it was a routine practice by me to vigilantly inspect the interior of the privy in daylight just to be sure. This 'little house' was located in a quiet place of serenity and relative seclusion so you could conduct your private business in peace, except for the porcine cacophony of irritating noises from our neighbour's pigs nearby on the opposite side of the boundary fence. Such was life at home in the bush.

There is a remarkably similar comparison between our particular circumstances in the early 50s and those rural hardships experienced by earlier Langwarrin resident Dorothy Capon, whose salient memories are recounted before and after 1925 as published by Dot Morrison in her book *Langwarrin Settlers and Soldiers* as follows:

> ...Everyone had to catch their water from their roof in iron tanks...In the early days washing was done outside. A brick place held the copper with firewood under it to boil the water... Coolgardie safes were made of flywire mesh... keeping the contents cool. No phone, no electricity; lights were kerosene lamps and candles...As the years went by [after 1925]... a chip heater to heat the water, coming from tanks. The toilet was a small room outside, a long way from the house.[2]

The site selected for our new house was at the rear of the large block, affording optimum privacy away from Cranbourne Road, which would eventually become the main thoroughfare for the district. The site only had one major obstacle: a massive mature conifer tree growing on the location. After many weeks of intensive hand excavation by shovel, pick and crowbar, chopping of the tree's roots by axe, and an immense amount of manual sawing using a two-man crosscut saw, the tree was ultimately removed. This left a gaping deep excavation much like a Second World War bomb crater. The foundations for the house had been established.

Although my father provided most of the physical work in removing this gigantic tree from our chosen house site, it was still a family project and we all helped where necessary. I distinctly recall being on the other end of the two-man saw on occasion, probably assisted by my sister, and being exhausted after just a few minutes' activity. As my father was a smoker who rolled his own cigarettes of Champion Ruby fine cut tobacco with Tally-Ho rolling papers in a small cigarette tube, it would be common for him to stop work just to prepare his cigarette.

He was not alone. In Australia in 1955, 40 per cent of Australian smokers rolled their own.[3] My father continued this habit for the remainder of his life and avoided the filter-tip cigarettes that were to become so fashionable in later years. Fortunately for me, his subsequent passing interest in cigars did not occur during this early rugged phase of the establishment of our house.

In those early days, communication with the outside world was via telephone with the nearest red public telephone box located at least one half mile away (0.8 kilometres), by hand-delivered telegrams for urgent messages, and by listening to the radio. Television (TV) only commenced transmission in Australia in late 1956, and we did not purchase a set until 1961. This was because as well as the cost of purchasing the television, there was also a TV licence fee required from the State Government, renewable annually, that could be difficult to afford by a family with limited income. Radio sets provided news events, nightly entertainment through quiz shows, adventure and drama serials, comedy shows and many other programs as well as music.

My most memorable shows included highly entertaining quiz programs by the popular radio announcer Jack Davey who always opened with his trademark enduring call sign of 'Hi! Ho! Everybody!', and intriguing adventure serials like *Hop Harrigan, Pacific Patrol* and *Dick Tracy*. Later into the evening, there were unusual programs such as *The Goon Show*, lively comedies like *Life with Dexter*, and scary radio plays about science fiction or horror stories. It was an era where radio entertainment ruled supreme, and listeners were spoiled for choice. I particularly liked shows requiring participants provide answers to quiz questions, guess the secret sound or perhaps provided comical feedback from real people. Keith Smith's local radio show *The Pied Piper* provided hilarious and candid responses from interviews with children.

Every evening after our main meal, the entire family gathered around the radio as their daily means of news and entertainment. Of course, we also had a gramophone record player for 12 inch (30 centimetre) long-playing vinyl records, but it was rarely used. The radio usually provided the essential diversity and choice for our young family, and unlike the early TV sets, was a relatively unobtrusive device. Although our radiogram combined the radio and the record player in a sleek cabinet, it was actually larger than a television due to a substantial output speaker. However, it always looked just like another piece of furniture and was an integral part of our living room, being finished in smart walnut-teak veneer panelling.

When it came to popular mainstream music in Australia, if it was not played on the radio, I probably never heard it. Record shops were not the place to hear the latest music releases in the 1950s. It was commercial radio that transmitted the vibes. In 1954, I adored *Hey There* by Rosemary Clooney. By 1956, it was the melancholic *Just Walkin' in the Rain* sung by every female teenager's heart throb and songwriter Johnnie Ray that was played incessantly in our country. One of my favourite tunes in 1957 as a six-year-old was the American folk song *Freight Train* by country artist Rusty Draper. In 1958, Australia's favourite was the highly successful and catchy Italian song/ballad *Nel blu dipinto di blu* (translated as 'In the blue that is blue') and popularly known as *Volare* (To fly). By 1959, it was the slow romantic tune traditionally played at secondary school graduation balls *Smoke Gets in Your Eyes* by the American rhythm and blues vocal group The Platters that ruled the Australian air waves.[4] In so many ways, these laconic and wistful songs reflected the period of slowly changing life in our nation. Rock 'n' roll music and Elvis Presley were about to be unleashed in the early 1960s when vinyl records would then dominate the marketplace.

Prior to the eventual introduction of television in our house at the start of 1961, the family participated in an immense variety of interesting and challenging board and card games at home such as Monopoly, Scrabble, Treasure Island, snakes and ladders and others. There were highly entertaining fun card games such as happy families or snap, or the more thoughtful checkers ('draughts') or dominoes. For the more adventurous, playing cards were used for somewhat serious pursuits such as whist, gin rummy, 500, pontoon or solitary patience. These board and card games may sound incredibly dull and unchallenging compared to today's choices of technological entertainment, but they were very popular prior to television.

It was all about having uncomplicated fun purely for the sake of your enjoyment, and usually involved most of the family. Oddly, even though the only scheduled transport system in our local district was actually a private bus service (Phillips' Buses) which operated infrequently between suburban Frankston and rural Cranbourne, one never felt the need to travel very far from home in those days. As a consequence, we often walked the three miles to Frankston for shopping excursions and took a bus home, such was the prevailing spirit of those times.

Of course, I developed personal interests for my own entertainment; most notably assembling jigsaw puzzles and completing colouring books that were very popular in the 50s. Jigsaw puzzles were perplexing and time-consuming which made them all the more interesting. They were usually given as a present and came in a colourful box illustrating the completed diagram. If only it was that simple. Once the hundreds of individual pieces were laid out on a table, trying to interlink them in a methodical way rarely ever finished successfully. Hours passed and absurd shapes were formed and then disassembled before complete frustration arose. Key pieces appeared to be missing and were then found lying on the floor. Eventually, once nearing completion, someone would rearrange the table and the entire assembled jigsaw puzzle would be lost.

Colouring books on the other hand came in a vast range of sizes and compositions, and required a quality set of coloured pencils on hand. The English Derwent pencils were always expensive but provided a fantastic range of subtle hues and shades of every complexion for an aspiring artist like me. I initially started with a modest starter set of 24 pencils and simply added individual colour pencils over several years. Who could possibly believe that there were 72 possible versions of different colour in the standard set of the time? It certainly made colouring a thoroughly enjoyable pastime.

The ongoing saga of building our own family home was a combination of negligible finances, ageing parents, and the relative difficulty of procuring building products in those days in our district. We eventually resorted to an accomplished local builder and somewhat popular identity in the district called Bert Murray to continue the process in several stages over the ensuing years, yet the prolonged delay had virtually no effect on the quality of our lives. This chap was far more than simply a handyman, and had a thoroughly deserved reputation for quality of work and versatility. As well as a carpenter, he was a welder, saw-miller, fabricator, poultry farmer and interestingly, an inventor. We knew that the home would be built to last without any unnecessary shortcuts given his all-round expertise, and eventually, the house was completed to satisfy our requirements by the 1960s.

Surprisingly, we were not alone in the nation regarding accommodation. An interesting public commentary on the perceived shortage of suitable accommodation available in rural Australia by 1956 is outlined in the following article concerning country pubs:

> … In any country town, there were as yet no motels, no well-advertised boarding houses, no such things as youth hostels. The only place for the weary traveller was the local pub… whatever it was you wanted from such an institution, it was missing. Well, almost. You get a bed and blankets. There was one toilet, down the hallway in the bathroom, with the leaking hand-basin, and a much-used bar of Sunlight soap. Not much else. Anyway, who does *actually* need a towel?

> These luxuries were not backed up by any display of cleanliness, and civility from the publican was in short supply… conditions in a great majority of cases are sub-standard. Beds are uncomfortable, evening meal hours ridiculous, and bath and lavatory [toilet] conditions in many cases insanitary and a menace to health.
>
> The only improvement of note in many hotels in recent years has been the provision of *inner-spring mattresses*. This labour-saving device avoids the need for shaking or turning the mattress…[5]

The mid-1950s were probably best known for the plethora of new domestic appliances and unusual gadgets marketed in Australia for providing greater comfort to consumers (particularly housewives) who demanded easier means to reduce the daily burden of their manual chores. We always had a Singer sewing machine out of necessity for mending and alteration of family clothing, but no electric automatic washing machine, vacuum cleaner, heating or cooling appliances, electric steam iron or fancy kitchen gadgets.

Perhaps my mother was not convinced of their necessity from the full page newspaper and colourful glossy magazine advertisements for these rather expensive items that depicted owning such appliances as glamorous and housewives as relaxed and satisfied. After all, there was nothing quite like 'elbow grease' (vigorous exertion) and improvisation to get a job done without spending any money. Sensibly, the new house only had polished wooden floor boards rather than carpeting, eliminating the need for a vacuum cleaner. However, the floors still needed to waxed and polished by hand, and routinely swept with a broom.

This responsibility was delegated to me as the youngest in the family and I embraced it with vigour. For my own exercise from about eight years of age onwards, I would stand on a discarded woollen cardigan or jumper in bare feet for better grip and then briskly slide/skate across the floorboards, thereby efficiently polishing the floor. However, sometimes in my exuberance, my slide would be too prolonged or have too much momentum over the slippery floorboards, resulting in an unfortunate airborne collision with an armchair or table. This was not the best way to complete the task but certainly had some entertaining outcomes for those watching my antics. By 12 years of age, I was now a big boy and far too old for such childish behaviour.

Eventually, through necessity, we purchased Australia's most famous vacuum cleaner; the upright Hoover Lark, best known by the advertising jingle 'It BEATS as it Sweeps as it Cleans'. It offered a revolution in carpet cleaning with an exclusive positive agitator to dislodge grit, a broad dirt finder to suck the grit and a dustproof capture bag. At its release in September 1956, the Hoover transformed vacuuming into an art form. It was 'a vacuum cleaner that was like no other, and a true suburban icon…'[3] Australians embraced the technology of vacuuming floors that became known by the colloquialism of 'doing the Hoovering'.[6]

One new outdoor appliance that we never owned but probably should have still sensibly purchased was a Hills Hoist height-adjustable rotary clothes line, for which an Australian patent was granted in 1956. Our family only ever had the old wire strung between two sturdy trees and propped for support of the wet clothing, which also served as a great perching location for native birdlife. The Hills Hoist iconic invention and National Treasure as listed by the National Library of Australia is still thriving in the modern era, and all started when the inventor's wife wanted a better clothes line. This remarkable technological development was to change everything and was so reliable that 'a Darwin family reported that the only thing left standing after Cyclone Tracy was their Hills Hoist'.[7]

If that endorsement was not enough, the following commentary might suffice instead:

> Have you seen the new 'Hills Hoist Rotary Clothes Line'? If ever there was a blessing – a gift – offered to the housewife, it is surely this item. Made of galvanised iron it will last for years, and when the wind blows it's like a merry-go-round! No more snapped lines with washing on the ground, or broken clothes props with disastrous results. The children will love it! For all that … I'm sorry the clothes prop man has lost his job.[8]

Wildfires and Bonfires

Although our property was not a rambling estate, it was an integral part of the surrounding bushland and sometimes difficult to distinguish as a residential development. As a consequence, native and exotic animals as well as reptiles played a significant part in our daily lives. For self-sufficiency, we maintained a large brood of small bantam hens, the ubiquitous white chickens and the odd Rhode Island Red rooster, and thus always had ample supplies of eggs and fresh chicken on the menu.

Figure 10: The chooks in 1954

You also never overslept in the morning with that rooster around. A pet nanny-goat was eventually procured for keeping the yard shipshape and the grass/weeds under control, as well as for providing luscious milk. Chickens and a goat were an excellent means for recycling food scraps and great companions as well for the children.

As I reflect on those times in the 50s, it seemed that virtually everyone was keeping a brood of hens on their properties, and the district was rife with poultry farms. Free range chickens were common and permitted to roam throughout each respective property in daylight hours, before being penned for the evening as foxes prevailed throughout the district. We always had a clutch of newly hatched chicks exploring our modest property and getting into mischief, but being so cute that everyone forgave their hilarious antics.

Native wildlife were frequent and inquisitive visitors to our property, ranging from spiny echidnas burrowing underground at short notice when disturbed, koalas lounging in selective eucalyptus trees, various large goanna lizards and innumerable snakes. Some reptiles were deadly and required the utmost caution, such as the terrifying tiger snake or the elusive but insidious copperhead snake that grew up to 5.6 feet (1.7metres) in length. My mother was usually assigned the task of tracking and removing the deadliest snakes from our place due to her tenacity and patience. I recall her once diligently waiting about two hours for a copperhead snake to emerge from a small swamp/soak on the property before successfully trapping it. These venomous varieties were lethal and a real risk to young unsuspecting children.

On another occasion whilst I was wandering through dense undergrowth, I encountered a tiger snake which suddenly reared up in preparation to strike. Its wide head and strong muscular body enabled it to assume a cobra-like posture of a flattened, flared head and neck, and a raised body. These were clear signs that preceded attack. Standing about one metre from a fearsome reptile poised to strike was quite a frightening moment for me, given that I was only about ten or eleven years of age. For those few precarious seconds, neither of us moved, as if frozen in time. Then slowly and ever so cautiously, I backed away from the irate reptile one painstaking step at a time, permitting it the opportunity to turn and slither harmlessly away into the bushes. Most snakes are only responding in self-defence when approached or disturbed by people, but one also has to exercise extreme caution and vigilance around them.

Sometimes unfortunate circumstances arose which resulted in tragic outcomes. There were identical twin sisters living in Langwarrin in those times named Lorna and Lorraine Cavill whose father coached my junior under-16 cricket team for years. On their appearance alone, it was impossible to tell them apart, for they even had identical haircuts. It was only after each one had spoken that you distinguished their unique personalities. In 1971 after I had left the district to pursue employment, I learned that Lorraine had subsequently married and had been pushing her infant in a pram along a local road where there were no footpaths. A passing car drove over a snake crossing this road, flipping the reptile into the air whence it subsequently landed inside the pram. In her desperate attempts to remove the snake from endangering her baby, Lorraine was bitten. She eventually perished from those bites.

A typical species of aquatic wildlife that I encountered from time to time only appeared in winter months with significant rainfalls. As our property was well below the level of the adjacent main road, it was quite prone to minor flooding during such periods, with the excess run-off accumulating in a small, topographically-low depression known as 'the swamp'. This was located along a property boundary and over the years, acted as a natural catchment for excessive winter rains. As a young child, I would play around and in the swamp bare-footed as you did in those days, particularly during periods of considerable rain deluges. Streamlets of run-off would flow into the swamp and it was an exciting place to explore for a youngster.

On one such day and whilst still knee-deep in the shallows, something attached itself to one of my heels and the resultant pain was excruciating. Whilst wincing in severe pain, I instantly withdrew my foot from the water and spotted minute, shallow puncture marks in my heel. They were bleeding profusely. A moment later something brushed against my other leg. Without a second thought about what it might be, I leapt out of the water onto dry land. One look at those bleeding wounds told me that there was something decidedly nasty in the water. The bites resembled that inflicted by a reptile and with visions of being poisoned, I carefully observed the water where I had been standing.

It was then that a long, slender and dark snake-like object flashed through the flowing water in front of me. It was a large freshwater eel and it appeared very agitated. I had never encountered them on the property in the past, but that winter had generated considerable rainfall run-off into our small swamp. There were probably others swimming around but I had only managed to irritate that particular eel. They are very difficult creatures to catch, so I avoided being bare-footed standing in the swamp altogether and pursued other less perilous interests.

The swamp was also inhabited by a plethora of amphibious frogs and their incessant croaking noise at night sometimes drove me quite barmy. Depending upon the season and time of evening, the volume of croaking varied markedly. I simply learned to ignore the overall crescendo and remember that it was far more beneficial than being infested by incessant swarms of mosquitoes. In hindsight, the sheer numbers of such special creatures surely indicated how relatively healthy the local swampy area remained over the years, and acted as a great means of controlling the mosquito population. Even chasing the tadpoles could be entertaining at times, without even getting my feet wet.

Our proximity to the adjacent nature reserve resulted in a spectacular and prolific range of visiting native bird species, some of whom choose to nest in the roof spaces of our home. On occasion, they would share these spaces with the local possums, and those mammals could certainly drum up some activity at night, scurrying around and under the roof, or leaping onto nearby tree branches. Keeping these inquisitive mammals from falling into our precious rainwater tank meant a constant state of vigilance for me.

For an entirely different type of wildlife experience, it would be difficult to surpass 'Cracker Night' held annually on 24th May preceding the onset of winter to officially celebrate 'Empire Day'. This date was Queen Victoria's birthday and after she died in 1901, Empire Day was assigned from 1902 to commemorate the monarch's memory in perpetuity. It was celebrated throughout the British Empire until the date was eventually renamed Commonwealth Day in 1958. Cracker Night was an important element of these celebrations as it meant bonfires, fireworks and a great family/community experience to people in the 50s, usually on a cold and sometimes foggy night.

I always commenced preparatory work on our property weeks before this special date by the diligent, progressive construction of a massive bonfire comprising dead tree branches and logs, disused cardboard boxes and as many old newspapers and magazines as could be sensibly scavenged. Fortunately, my mother kept a huge supply of the iconic *Australian Women's Weekly, Woman's Day, The New Idea* and some fashion magazines such as *Vanity Fair,* whilst Dad retained various rural publications, such as *The Countryman*. Almost all magazines and newspapers had enormously large page sheets by today's standards that when crumpled sufficiently made excellent combustible fuel sources. Tucking these crumpled sheets into every available space between branches and logs would certainly assist the fire.

The bonfire site was set well away from all buildings and trees in the middle of our cleared property, and slowly grew over the weeks from a few stacked branches into a massive mound several metres in height. Strategic placement of solid dried logs throughout guaranteed the fire burning for hours. As a final symbolic stage, I sometimes fabricated a ceremonial straw man resembling an effigy of Guy Fawkes in an old shirt, trousers, hat, and a head composed of compressed newspapers, and positioned it standing proudly atop the bonfire. Multiple layers of miniscule Tom Thumb firecrackers were secreted in the straw man's legs and arms, and a few large Penny Bungers resembling small sticks of dynamite stuck inside his head. All was ready for the bonfire night of the year.

In the 50s, the range of fireworks for public use was extensive and most affordable. Families purchased their stocks from variety stores individually (skyrockets, roman candles, Vesuvius fountains, Catherine wheels), by the handful such as firecrackers (Tom Thumbs, half-penny, penny, threepenny and the jumbo sixpenny bungers), or by the packet (short and long sparklers). For simplicity, they were defined as exploding fireworks such as crackers, colourful spectacular fireworks such as the innumerable candles, canisters, incendiary cones, pinwheels and luminescent sparklers, and the combination explosive/dazzling skyrockets.

On the evening, the family would gather around the bonfire and it would be lit at dusk at which time various loud crackers would be ignited. The smaller Tom Thumb layer of crackers were much like the repetitive sound of a machine gun operating, whereas the large 'bungers' were extraordinarily loud and placed at a considerable distance from fellow revellers. The sporadic booming noise as each bunger exploded was deafening. Sometimes the fuse of a cracker that had been lit by a match would splutter in the damp night air and stop burning. If there was enough fuse remaining, it was relit and eventually exploded. Other times, the fuse burnt down completely but the cracker never exploded, only to detonate a minute later without any warning. No-one would approach a cracker that had yet to fire until quite a time had elapsed.

A highlight of this activity one particular year was the ignition of the single jumbo sixpenny bunger purchased for the occasion. It was placed at the extremity of festivities and the family all stood on the far side of the bonfire. Fortunately it was ignited very early in the evening out of respect for our neighbour because it exploded like dynamite and literally left a small crater in the ground. 'Never again!' was the subsequent terse commandment issued by my mother. This activity was complemented by the straw man exploding shortly afterwards atop of the bonfire as the flames finally engulfed the effigy that vanished spectacularly in an almighty ball of fire.

As the night progressed and the bonfire grew in intensity, various colourful fireworks were slowly lit exhibiting a fantasia of vivid colours and incandescent sparks. These would be affixed to nearby fences or positioned on trees for maximum effect and there were many delightful displays. Sparklers would also be used to great effect by holding them in each hand and making imaginary shapes whilst dancing in the dark.

Figure 11: Backyard bonfire (© Shutterstock)

Later into the evening as the bonfire consolidated more into a log fire with intensely hot coals, it was time for the final closing stage of the celebrations using skyrockets. A range of skyrockets were individually placed in empty milk or beer bottles sitting on the ground, and the tinder paper lit on all of them. One by one or simultaneously, they streaked skywards before exploding in a sensational shower of colour and sparks. On the odd occasion, a skyrocket went astray and spiralled off course before exploding in nearby trees but this was rare indeed.

I am reminded of the following commentary of a rather adventurous night experienced by another participant of Cracker Night:

> One year, the richest kid in the neighbourhood brought all his crackers in a leather suitcase. He was going to save them till last. Then there was this enormous bang. The suitcase went about six feet in the air. There were rockets driving into the ground and catherine wheels spinning out of control, bungers going off like

gunfire. For a moment, the suitcase was silhouetted against the bonfire and then disintegrated in midair.[1]

Figure 12: Cracker Night (Ann Langdon)

Early the following morning whilst everyone else slept, I always conducted a reconnaissance survey of the site and retrieved various unexploded crackers, misplaced fireworks dropped in the dark and scattered unused sparklers. There would always be next year's bonfire after all.

Fortunately we did not own any pets in those days because animals have a distinctive dislike of loud explosive fireworks for very good reason. We did eventually inherit a lovely female cat in later years aptly nicknamed 'Crooked Head' caused by a prior unfortunate injury. This Tabby was so relaxed that it routinely rolled off seats or benches or anywhere else of height when it slept. We couldn't upset the family cat otherwise it only invited bad karma.

Sadly, the celebration of Empire Day complete with a massive bonfire and incredible fireworks has long since been consigned to history, and another similar night known as Guy Fawkes Night celebrated on 5th November in late Spring is now largely defunct in Australia. Many parts of Australia have banned or restricted the use of fireworks other than for significant 'official' events such as New Year's Eve or Australia Day. This has arisen from a fear of accidents, fires and injuries associated with fireworks and a lack of open spaces in suburbia for bonfires.[2]

As I grew older and started my secondary education as a teenager, my interests changed and Cracker Night ceased to be held on our property. Besides, no-one else in the family was sufficiently motivated to make those massive bonfires. Cracker Night and its magnificent bonfire will always live on in my memory as a special traditional custom when my family celebrated a fun night together and I had the rare opportunity to enjoy hands-on use of fireworks, particularly those loud bungers and the spectacular skyrockets – what an exciting, thoroughly magical night to behold!

Domestic Life

To appreciate the challenges facing a family with three children under eight years of age starting a new life on an undeveloped, semi-rural block of land with virtually no access to public utilities, it was first imperative to decide what was really important.

Unlike most Australian homes in the 50s, we did not have a backyard. Many homes in suburban areas were positioned towards the front of their property and closest to the adjoining road for ease of access by an automobile. As a consequence, they had small presentable front yards with manicured lawns or gardens, and large extended back yards with a diversity of additions, such as an outdoor laundry wash-house, a small woodshed or garden shed, a clothes line, an incinerator, a vegetable patch, some fruit trees and possibly a water tank.[1]

As our house was not in suburbia, it was built right beside the boundary fence at the rear of the property and furthermost from the main road at the front. There was no backyard, but we did have an extensive front yard stretching over an acre in area. Our property seemed almost indistinguishable from the surrounding pristine bushland, and given my prolonged exploratory travels around Langwarrin, I guess it was reasonable to conclude that the entire local district was my front yard.

Somehow we always managed to fit any additions into this yard without unnecessary clearing of the native vegetation, such as a chicken coop, an outdoor latrine, a wire-prop clothes line, laundry wash-tubs and copper, a limited selection of planted fruit trees, a herb garden and even a small lawn area for our nanny-goat. From my limited perspective as the youngest of the brood, the important things that mattered were the freedom to explore the local district, daily family life and of course, meal times.

My mother was versatile if not a battler. She prepared a meal from even the most basic ingredients, yet it was always nutritious and satisfying. Little did I realise that lamb's fry (various organ offal), tripe (edible lining of sheep's stomach) or sheep brains could be so good for me, as she stated so many times. Red meat was also on the menu using selective cuts and sometimes supplemented by local rabbit stew, chicken meat or hearty chicken broth cooked from the carcass. Vegetables were almost always baked and in plentiful supply as were salads. Field mushrooms gathered from outlying properties might be cooked if in-season, and they were often gigantic.

My mother was also a very astute shopper due to our modest finances, and she would generally select the discounted cuts of meat, marked or bruised fruit and vegetables, and bread on sale late in the day when it was heavily reduced in price. Her special adage was that 'too many people eat with their eyes' by disdaining food that did not look nice or perhaps in the case of fruit and vegetables, were in some way marked or bruised. The nutritional value and taste of food far outweighed that of its physical appearance or presentation. She could turn most food into various stews (such as apple and rhubarb), patties, soups, fruit cocktails and other concoctions without fancy names, but definitely tasty. Nothing was wasted, including food scraps that were recycled to the garden for fertiliser.

At different times between the end of summer and late autumn, field mushrooms suddenly appeared throughout our district, usually triggered by occasional rainy periods or heavy overnight dews. I might have been exploring bushland around the district one day, and the following day, these wonders of nature have sprouted out of the same ground without any prior indication. Paddock mushrooms (*Agaricus campestris*) and the huge horse mushrooms (*Agaricus avensis*) were always easy to distinguish as the only edible types, with every other mushroom treated either as potentially poisonous or as a toadstool, and thus left in the ground. I recall coming home from one such early morning exploratory mission with mushrooms so large that I could only really carry about a dozen. When cooked for breakfast with free range eggs or added to steak as a thick mushy sauce, field mushrooms were extra special.

Our bread was exclusively wholemeal in those days when it was originally still 'whole grain', and butter ruled supreme as heart-healthy margarine was yet to gain acceptance as a substitute. Full cream milk, free range eggs and bacon, bulk porridge and grain cereals comprised a normal breakfast. Black tea was brewed in a porcelain pot rather than from a teabag, and usually required coarse brown sugar and cream just to lessen the distinctively bold and sharp taste.

Black tea certainly had a well deserved place in our Australian culture. From its earliest beginnings when served as 'billy' tea using boiling water heated in a small, portable metal bucket or can ('a billy') over a campfire and garnished with a twig of eucalyptus leaves for flavouring, a 'cuppa' of dry leaf tea was the hot beverage of choice for most adult Australians in the 1950s. This was until the appearance of granulated instant coffee (just add hot water). However, it was the ritual of brewing the tea diligently that was critical to the palate, as indicated by the following commentary compiled from passionate Australian lovers of tea in this era:

> I am a chronic tea-drinker and I think it runs in the family. My father has been accused of bathing in tea, so much of it does he consume.
>
> Very conservatively, I figure that we have consumed a total of 260,000 cups of tea so far in our lifetime … some of your correspondents ill-treat the beverage to the extent of stewing it for five and even 10 minutes.
>
> There is only one way to drink tea – while it is hot, and before it changes from a delicacy to a powerful tanning agent.
>
> We have both found that one minute is the ideal brewing time. Ten minutes' tea brewing should be included in the capital offences. (Letters, C.M.)[2]

Dessert was a real treat for me and included unflavoured 'Greek style' yoghurt (now labelled 'natural' yoghurt), fresh local blackberries overgrowing our neighbour's fence, or stewed plums, rhubarb, apples or prunes, and of course, home-baked apple pie. Perhaps once a month, vanilla ice-cream from a cardboard carton or freshly whipped cream was added for more flavour for our palates. For some unknown reason, my mother never purchased flavoured ice-cream which only came in one choice anyway.

Neapolitan (harlequin) ice-cream comprised three separate blocks of chocolate, vanilla and strawberry side by side in the same cardboard container, permitting you to enjoy each flavour individually. I suspect as flavoured ice-creams were relatively uncommon in Australia in the 50s, people had few options. Of course this precluded continental ice-creams, such as the expensive Italian gelato varieties purchased at selective venues, such as at the annual Royal Melbourne Show for example. My favourite Italian ice-cream was the layered fruit and nut cassata or cherry Tartufo.

Between meals in summer, it was also possible to glean a sweet treat from the refrigerator (in the 1960s) by making ice cubes enhanced with coloured cordial or tasty jelly crystals in the freezer compartment of the refrigerator. Although unlike nearby Frankston, we did not have daily home deliveries of pasteurised milk in glass bottles direct from the dairy, so we had to improvise. A visit once to a local farm in our district resulted in several large containers of freshly produced full cream milk direct from the cows. It was delicious to say the least.

Interestingly, the same farm also had an infestation of rabbits and on a rare subsequent visit, I was invited by the farmer to join him on a local cull. Keen to impress my mother with fresh rabbit for our evening meal, I trotted along with the farmer with his caged ferrets in hand. After releasing a ferret into a prospective burrow, it would be my responsibility to trap any rabbit chased from the hideaway using a small net placed across the exit. This was a particularly tricky operation, as wild rabbits were deceptively fast when chased by a ferret. There were also possibly other exits from each burrow.

On my third attempt, I finally captured a feral rabbit before the farmer took over the task. Not a bad effort for a nine-year-old. Delighted with my catch, I returned home with quite a plump prize, only to realise that during the rabbit hunt, I had been traversing local scrub that had been recently scorched by a bush fire. As a result, I was covered in black soot and my clothing was criss-crossed with innumerable black charcoal markings from brushing against the burnt vegetation. Although the rabbit was gratefully accepted for a hearty stew as our evening meal, my reward was being sent to bed early for being in such a state, as was to be expected.

For tea breaks during most days at home, we only ever had broken plain or sweet biscuits. Most people purchased unbroken biscuits, and so any casualties were typically stored in gigantic biscuit tins and then wrapped in brown paper bags for sale (prior to the days of sealed packaging). These 'damaged' biscuits were not acceptable to many, and sold at about half the price of unbroken ones while still tasting exactly the same. By 1955, packaging was becoming the new way to market groceries in smaller convenient sizes and weights for consumers, and of course, everything became more expensive in return. Cereals and flour in packets, beans and condensed milk in cans, and bottled milk were making their way onto grocery shelves. 'There was even talk that bread would come wrapped in paper, while on the other hand, meat might soon not be wrapped in newspaper, but in white unused paper.'[3]

My mother sometimes also baked cream sponge cakes. The additional bonus to this culinary delight was being the chosen youngster selected to clean/lick the hand-cranked, wire whisk mixer (known as an 'egg beater') used to manually whip the cream and combine powdered cocoa or chocolate into the mixture. Not a trace of cream or cocoa would remain on the mixer's whisk after my close attention.

The manual egg beater was not a fancy appliance despite its impressive manufacturer's title as the 'Persinware silent drive Rotary Beater No.39'. It offered a comfortable grip handle with a thoughtful thumb rest, silent effortless operation due to its nylon gears, and non-splash, stainless steel blades for longer life. It was also sold in glorious colours of black, primrose, blue, red, green or ivory, at the reasonable price of 19 shillings and sixpence, or just under 30 dollars in equivalent value in 2016.[4,5]

Whilst on the subject of meal times, the nightly meal had a non-negotiable attendance deadline of 6 pm, no matter what plausible excuse was provided. In one case when I limped home late due to a misadventure with a rogue Border Collie dog who latched onto my leg, it was off to bed without any meal. I think that I was around nine to ten years of age and indestructible at the time. This punishment was ultimately circumvented when I agreed to chop twice as much firewood the following day. Discipline was paramount in our family for very good reason. As youngsters, we all needed strong guidance, and misbehaviour such as unacceptable (foul) language always met with rigid punishment. Sometimes the threat of corporal punishment was a sufficient deterrent rather than the act itself. For example, if you were caught swearing, it would be washing-out your mouth with whatever soap was handy. In our home, the iron fist ruled all.

Remedial elixirs and potions were rampant through the 1950s, with every conceivable size of glass jar of powder and liquid (before aerosols), or tube of cream on the health market actively promoted for potentially curing or preventing almost every medical affliction known to mankind. We did not have a first aid cabinet at home, but rather an entire bathroom of medications to heal and manage most injuries, ailments or anything else medical. It was an era when a chemist shop was more an apothecary, although some medications were still purchased in variety stores, and you only visited a doctor when all the home remedies had failed or an injury was quite serious.

My parents had the same family doctor in Frankston for at least forty years until he passed away. This doctor dispensed crucial medicines, provided immunisation injections for serious childhood illnesses, and sometimes rarely mended broken limbs.

> The parents of the baby boomers were a generation who had lost brothers and sisters in infancy. This left them with an anxiety about their own children's health, although happily, they could be fairly confident of rearing them to adulthood. They had faith in science, but not quite enough to abandon their folk wisdom.[6]

Both my mother and father always preferred the various potions, concoctions and numerous 'natural' remedies as the first line of medical defence to a doctor's visit. Whether it was the expense or the distance to his Frankston surgery, my parents almost always chose the traditional family remedy over modern science. Fortunately, when it came to measles, mumps and chickenpox, the doctor always knew best.

Our family routinely utilised a combination of both manufactured elixirs and natural ingredients, like castor oil and cod liver oil for digestive health, and lanolin cream for skin healing. In no particular order, I recall Friars' Balsam for treating colds, Vicks VapoRub salve for relieving nasal and chest congestion and Lane's Emulsion (cod liver oil with many other ingredients and orange flavoured) for digestive health and wellbeing. For soft tissue ailments, there was Faulding's Zinc Cream for problem skin, Calamine Lotion for sunburn and insect bites, Sloan's Liniment for temporary relief of muscle or joint pain, Mecurochrome antiseptic liquid for abrasions and Savlon antiseptic cream for cuts and wounds.

Each had their own particular health benefits and sometimes distinctive qualities, such as an extraordinarily strong fishy smell or taste, a distinctive antiseptic smell common to hospitals, or perhaps stained your clothing. Who could ever forget the medical liquid Sloan's Liniment that came in a small and flat clear glass bottle with the face of its inventor proudly displayed on the label and the encouraging words 'KILLS PAIN'. The bottle resembled a hip flask for alcohol and the liquid smelled like hospital antiseptic, but it always worked successfully. After vigorously rubbing it into the afflicted area, a few minutes later the pain was gone, although I always had an aroma like a sterile hospital ward for days afterwards. It became a mainstay of our family's medicinal collection.

To properly relieve a chest/nasal congestion required adding a generous portion of Vicks VapoRub to a dish of very hot water, and keeping my head over the dish covered with a small towel. After several prolonged minutes of deep inhalation, my breathing certainly became far easier. As a final solution, rubbing the decongestant over my chest just before going to sleep at night completed the therapy. This era was well before the days of the myriad of commercial sunscreen solutions now available, and zinc cream (with a key ingredient of zinc oxide) was commonly in use for facial protection from sunburn and windburn whilst at the beach.

This was greatly assisted by many lifesavers adopting it as their preferred method of sun protection, and became one of the most enduring products to symbolise 'the Australian way of life'. Not only was it waterproof, but even by today's standards, zinc cream offered the maximum protection against broad spectrum ultraviolet rays with an actual SPF (Sun Protection Factor) rating of about 30, yet it can only be marketed as SPF 15+.[7]

Natural remedies were always preferred in our home, from using fresh honey and lemons in managing sore throats to consuming hot black tea for headaches. Aspirin analgesics were used sparingly, and only if someone had intense pain or a high temperature. It was rare for any of our family to incur a serious illness or injury and I deduce this was because we simply got on with our lives and did not dwell on minor ailments, bumps or scratches. As the familiar adage went; 'there is always someone worse off than you', and I imagined that somehow this would always be the case.

However, sometimes this was not the case and medicine from a pharmacy was essential, such as when I was constipated. For this cure, there was 'The Laxette Way'. This remedy came in a box of 24 tiny squares of tempting milk chocolate containing the gentle, tasteless and natural laxative senna, made specifically for children and guaranteed by the manufacturer to make me well again overnight. I had no doubt that they would be effective and would resolve the problem which may have been causing me to be 'crabby, naughty or nervy' as the manufacturer suggested. This was of course unless too many yummy chocolate-flavoured squares were consumed...

I rarely ever tried them again after that harrowing experience and relied instead upon more natural remedies, such as eating a surfeit of plums.

Sometimes, a childhood ailment appeared that was beyond the healing powers of family potions and elixirs. It might be the spread of warts on your hands or a persistent cough that never quite went away. That is when a visit to 'a medical specialist' usually based in Melbourne ensued, and a lengthy course of exotic creams or tablets undertaken. I never minded the distraction as it meant a day trip to the city by train, usually a delicious large cooked lunch, and missing school.

Whether my sense of humour assisted me through the many difficult learning experiences of family discipline and injury management is still unclear to me, but I certainly appreciated the right values gained in life's journey – honesty, hard work and fairness to all. On one weekend, I was asked by a neighbour to help with hay baling on their farm for a few hours, earning the princely sum of £5 or 100 shillings for my efforts. This was a fortune by today's values in 2016 of an equivalent of almost $140, especially for a young person whose weekly pocket money would rarely exceed one shilling and an incredible financial windfall for an 11-year-old.[8] Despite handing over the money upon returning home, I was sent to bed without a meal anyway for not first seeking parental permission to undertake the hay baling which was considered relatively dangerous work. The young entrepreneur was thwarted yet again by home rules.

My father's generosity somewhat compensated me for this misdemeanour by a shopping trip to nearby Frankston the next day, and a splurge on confectionery. A visit to one of the large variety stores in town was all that I needed to recover from my punishment. The choice of lollies on display along the counters was phenomenal, with individual compartments containing various toffees, liquorice, boiled lollies, caramels, wrapped sweets, nougat blocks and even sticky honeycomb. After selecting virtually everything, we headed home with me tightly clutching my lollies in little white paper bags. However on reaching home, I soon realised that my reward would be short-lived, and sure enough, the remaining sweets were confiscated to be rationed later, subject to my behaviour. After all, dental hygiene was paramount and too many sweets meant tooth decay and a dreaded visit to the dentist.

Daily life on our property was never dull throughout the 50s.The construction of the family home extended over most of the decade and beyond, never really being entirely completed. My father's advanced age and deteriorating health with the passing years meant sections of the house remained only partially completed until well after his passing in 1964. Dad's main interest was in being an artist, and he painted and sketched throughout his lifetime, of which I still have wonderful enduring memories. He was a well-travelled man prior to starting our family, and had a comprehensive gift for painting landscapes, seascapes and locales visited around the world and in Australia, as well as sketching incisive caricatures of various people in charcoal or using HB lead pencils.

Figure 13: Various caricatures of the day

Dad specialised in bringing his subject matter to life in sketches through unusual expressions or deft use of water colours in his paintings, and from time to time would convene public exhibitions of his artworks. In 1952, he held an exhibition of water colour paintings predominantly of Australian locales, as well as from Asia, Europe and Egypt. I vaguely recall another exhibition actually held at our property inside a large canvas marquee in November 1955 when mostly his Australian art was displayed as well as selective antiques. The event even made the local monthly news sheet *The Langwarrin News* which was only ever issued over the 1955-56 period, and was delivered by volunteers; '… An exhibition of watercolour paintings and antiques is to be held at the King's home, on Cranbourne Road, opposite *Cruden Farm*'.[9] His generous and caring nature endeared him to others, and I am reminded of his behaviour towards a stranger who visited our property one day.

Travelling gypsies and itinerant swagmen/vagabonds would occasionally pass through our district in the 50s in search of casual employment (chopping firewood, baling hay and performing odd jobs) or perhaps simply seeking a meal, so it was not unexpected that we would receive such a visit eventually. The rest of the family was away either at school or shopping that day when just such a lone traveller arrived and was greeted by my father. I am unsure what transpired between them, but when my mother eventually returned home later that day, the stranger had left with a gift donated by my father – one of his precious artworks. Although my mother was irate at such an overly generous gesture, Dad offered the swagman something only an artist would offer to help a battler on life's journey.

I always felt for those homeless wanderers in tattered clothing with their meagre possessions rolled in a swag bedroll of blankets and often carrying a tucker bag for food and a billy for boiling water. Such nomads with limited belongings walked the country in pursuit of any menial task offering meals and shelter, never staying long enough to call anywhere home. In some ways, their freedom was to be envied, with no constraints other than finding each day's basic necessities. Each night in the bush, they slept next to a campfire or perhaps in some man-made structure, such as under a bridge or a barn. It was rare to encounter them in the district, possibly because they avoided nearby Frankston and its urban sprawl.

We were also to be visited by a small group of gypsies in the mid-1950s, riding horses no less and towing an unusual wagon as their mobile accommodation. The visit was somewhat brief for although I was fascinated by their colourful costumes and animated behaviour, my mother was unimpressed and wary of these travellers and of their reputation. They continued on their journey without staying for long, and did not return. There was always something happening in our district to keep one fully occupied.

I distinctly recall a bushfire which raged through our local area on Cranbourne Road in the early 60s during one particularly hot summer in which I assisted by fighting the fire carrying a portable water-spray kit on my back. The volunteer fire brigade was always seeking locals to assist, but when my mother saw me covered in black soot and filthy from the smoke, such participation became strictly off-limits for this teenager thereafter. The local brigade was also seeking new recruits at the time, but once my mother decided on the matter, there was no further discussion required.

Even though our home was not too distant from Frankston, it was still relatively isolated, with only a limited bus service operating through the district from Monday to Saturday. As a consequence, we rarely had visitors from outside Langwarrin, except on rare occasions. Unusually, one of my mother's oldest female friends decided to visit us unannounced on a Sunday afternoon in the late 1950s. The lady lived in Richmond, one of the original inner suburbs closest to Melbourne, and a considerable distance of 43 kilometres from Langwarrin. It was not simply a direct route. First she had to get two different buses to the nearest railway station, the train to Frankston and then walk the remaining five kilometres to our house. As I recall, she was given a lift part of the way by a passing vehicle.

Public train and bus services in the metropolitan area on a Sunday were most infrequent, often an hour apart between scheduled departures, and sometimes finishing in the early evening on specific bus routes. When our visitor eventually departed for home, it was late in the afternoon around 4 pm and involved her walking towards Frankston, anticipating another lift from a passing vehicle, and then catching the next available train. Her last connecting bus to reach her house in Richmond left around 8 pm. The carefree spirit of such people to reach their destination by any possible means so typified this golden era. The lady later informed my mother that she had eventually arrived home around 9 pm after an extensive five hour journey. Quite an adventurous and independent lady in so many respects.

Child's Play and Festivities

When you had to make your own fun in those days, it helped enormously to have an enormous Cootamundra wattle tree growing on your property. The branches of this old tree were ideal to construct a rudimentary tree-house or 'cubby' precariously perched high in its foliage, and for erecting a swing. The swing was made from sturdy thick rope tied around a disused tyre at one end and the other end swung from the strongest branch. I would climb through the suspended tyre and sit resting both feet on the ground. By pushing fiercely with my feet, the swing quickly gained momentum, but if I really wanted to swing as high as possible, my sister did all the pushing instead.

Between us, we spent hours in that rickety tree-house with such a magnificent view of the surrounding bush and well above the world below. It remained off-limits on particularly windy days when the tree swayed uncontrollably and the structure seemed very fragile. When the wattle flowered towards the end of winter and into spring, there was a magnificent display to behold of masses of resplendent yellow blooms, and yet one that only lasted for a few precious weeks each year.

Climbing trees seemed to become a very natural hobby for me over the years, and I certainly became adept, given the dense stand of massive conifer (pine) trees growing at our boundary fence in the nearby nature reserve. It was nothing to clamber up even the tallest pine trees for the best views of the district and simply listen to the breeze as it wafted through the branches of pine needles. Better still was to see how far I could crawl out on a major branch in a strong wind to see if I could survive the extreme swaying motion of that branch by maintaining a very tight grip. Who needed to ride a roller coaster at a fun park or a wild bull at a rodeo compared to a large pine tree in the wind? I probably needed quite a sound sense of balance when scaling large trees, and this may have assisted me in eventually learning to ride a bicycle at home. Although we never owned bicycles as a family, I recall resurrecting an old one left disused in one of the bungalows and practised for many hours trying to master it as a 13-year-old.

Figure 14: The Cootamundra wattle

I found a gentle slope on the property, pushed the bike by its handle bars and jumped onto the rider's seat without pedalling until crashing into a tree or some other object. Eventually, I learned to operate the pedals just before crashing again. Finally after days of perseverance, I mastered the technique and actually rode the bicycle without crashing. That sense of balance was just so very important and the only way to avoid all those scratches and bruises. I also learned to become expert at patching tyre inner tubes with those vulcanising heat patches that burned so intensely once ignited. Then to spoil the fun, someone invented fast drying adhesive to replace it and virtually overnight eliminated another favourite pastime.

It may have been one of life's simplest pleasures for a child in the 50s, but playing in the dark always brought back many fond memories for me. Typically after finishing your evening meal between 6 pm and 7 pm, it was either off to bed or be seated in front of the radiogram listening to regular family serial programs. On the odd occasion on weekends, this unwritten rule was relaxed, and the children could stay up much later.

When it was a cloudless and calm night with a full moon, the property took on quite an eerie look from the extensive shadows generated by moonlight flooding through the local foliage and stands of taller trees. It created the perfect setting for my sister and I to play various pursuit games by the light of the moon. Hide and seek was particularly enjoyable, as long as you avoided moving into the moonlit areas. Another challenging game was to be the first to get from the house at the rear of the block to the main road at the front of the property and back again without leaving the shadows. This was an extremely difficult feat where there was only limited foliage to create shadows. If you inadvertently stepped into the direct moonlight, the game was over.

Add the effects of a light evening breeze causing the foliage branches to sway and the resultant shadows to subtly shift and merge, and it became quite a challenge to remain within the shadows. If the breeze increased to a gusty wind, it was impossible to successfully complete the perilous journey. My imagination seemed to be limitless at night when conjuring new games to play in the darkness. It was almost as if my personal freedom was no longer bounded by that rigid set of rules imposed by parents on their young children during daylight hours. What an extreme relief it was to simply be myself on such occasions.

I would be remiss not to mention another peculiar feature of the night applicable to young children over countless past generations, and that was of the mythical bogeyman or boogie man. It was always instilled in me in those early years about this supposedly horrible, malevolent and fiendish creature or spirit that mysteriously lurked somewhere in the darkness until I misbehaved and then emerged to inflict suitable punishment. The recounting of the fairy tale varied slightly depending upon the extent of my misbehaviour, but the outcome always had the same fatalistic end for a naughty child. I can think of only one worse punitive outcome and that was clearly detailed in the following sentiment: 'Just wait until your father comes home.'

Although the source of this fearsome and terrifying character was actually imaginary, it was real to any youngster who had to visit the outhouse at night with only a flickering hurricane lantern to light the way. Worse still, perhaps the visit to this 'little house' was necessary during a stormy night when trees were creaking in the wind, and the wind was howling through the overhead branches that were scratching violently on the roof. Let me tell you, the return journey to the house was more like an Olympic dash through the darkness than a casual stroll. If the purpose of recounting this fairy tale was to instil fear and trepidation about bad behaviour, it certainly worked on me.

Even the definition of a bogey translates into dread as follows:

> … A terrifying spirit of English folklore, of uncertain, but probably hobgoblinish nature, thought of as an 'it'… a 19th century word, probably derived from words meaning terror, ghost or hobgoblin [a source (often imagined) of fear or trouble].[1]

The game of 'shadows' with my classmates at primary school was far more subdued than that played at home on a moonlit night with my sister. It was played in bright sunshine and was all about preventing anyone else from standing or stomping on your shadow. Someone was initially selected as the game's chaser (also known as 'It') and the remaining group of children would then do their utmost to avoid their shadows 'being caught'. By moving ever so slightly when approached by the chaser, I mostly avoided

Fig. 15: Suburban backyard bogeyman

having my shadow being caught, unless it became too congested on the school's playground and I eventually collided with others in total panic. The winner was the last person remaining not to have their shadow caught. Of course, the game really became frenetic and the minor collision injuries escalated when there were two chasers involved in the relentless pursuit.

Another favourite children's pastime of mine was skipping games. I freely acknowledge up front that skipping ropes were strictly the domain of girls in the 1950s, and they were experts in every possible child's game with them. Unlike the immensely popular hula hoop craze of this era that only required an individual to master the technique, skipping ropes often needed at least three participants to really enjoy; a child holding the wooden handle at opposite ends of the rope and the third to skip over the rope. My sister was so proficient that she could skip and briskly turn a shorter skipping rope on her own, then invite me to join her to skip together. This required incredible concentration and co-ordination, yet our synchronisation was perfect. She could also skip alternatively between two ropes being turned by two classmates standing nearby.

With a much longer skipping rope available at my primary school and two children turning it, various classmates would progressively enter and skip the rope. The contest was to start with one child skipping and keep increasing the number slowly without catching on the moving rope. I recall our record was about six to eight people skipping in synchronisation before somebody faltered. Children could also leave the skipping group if becoming exhausted by jumping out of the rope area and re-enter later. What an amazing sight watching several children so co-ordinated that they could all skip simultaneously over the rope without falling or stumbling.

Of course, the two children turning the skipping rope maintained the same rhythm throughout. For something different, they would increase the rate of turning the rope briefly, resulting in the combined skipping group having to jump the rope faster and faster until eventually stumbling on the rope. Chanting a suitable counting-out rhyme was another useful method to maintain the entire skipping rhythm in an orderly fashion and signal when a participant could enter or leave the skipping group by spelling the last word of 'O-U-T'. I cannot recall those specific rhymes and rely upon the diligence of renowned American scholar Dorothy Howard and her pioneering research in the mid-1950s of Australian children's playground activities to select an appropriate skipping chant:

> Donald Duck he had no sense
> He bought a fiddle for eighteen pence
> Try as he might he could not play
> His beak got in the way
> And O-U-T spells out.[2]

Only ball games were probably as popular a pastime as skipping and hopscotch at our primary school. It was always difficult to get a basketball, softball or football as they were always in use at play times, so a tennis ball was the next best alternative. They were lightweight, soft and easy to handle, reasonably inexpensive to purchase, and as soon as I produced one, everyone either wanted to join me or grab the ball for themselves. Impromptu cricket games were terrific with a tennis ball as I could sometimes hit the ball out of the school ground and catching it was easy as well. Even when the ball was being bowled and it struck the child who was batting, it did not hurt. Many a record number of runs was scored using this type of ball at lunch breaks. By winter and the ensuing cold, blustery weather conditions, everyone wanted to kick the football around and the poor tennis ball was consigned to the storage room. Girls were mainly interested in playing netball, and so activity using a tennis ball seemed to be restricted to small groups intent on bouncing them against a wall whilst chanting repetitive jingles or number counting rhymes.

Of all the festivities enjoyed in a year, nothing quite surpassed the Christmas period for me, except perhaps for my birthday parties. One way of keeping very busy traditionally occurred in the weeks preceding Christmas. As there was a plethora of small shrubby pine trees growing wild in the unpopulated native bushland behind our property, and because I always needed extra pocket money, the solution became obvious. Cranbourne Road was progressively handling increasing volumes of vehicular traffic into the late 50s and represented a great source of potential customers who may be interested in purchasing a small Christmas tree on their way home. The young entrepreneur was born. With a hand-written sale sign displayed along both ends of the road about one hundred metres from our driveway and a neat pile of freshly cut small pine trees prepared in the shade, the business was ready. To my way of thinking at the time, it actually served an environmental purpose by thinning out the dense proliferation of these smaller conifers because only a select few were taken for sale, permitting the remainder more space to satisfactorily develop into fully grown trees.

Prices varied between one shilling (10 cents) and two shillings sixpence (25 cents) dependent upon the size and shape of the tree. For an exceptional tree, the astronomical price of five shillings (50 cents) applied, but such trees were rare. In the first two years, business was brisk with most trees sold well before Christmas and only the occasional tree left by Christmas Eve. Rarely did a five shilling tree sell, such as when a man in a Jaguar sports car purchased it for ten shillings (one dollar) instead and told me to keep the change. Most people simply wanted a freshly cut tree at a reasonable price.

If anyone thought that this occupation was easy, try sitting around for hours throughout each day waiting for a car to stop and then having to barter with the driver over an agreed price. By the third year, I suffered stiff competition from my Dutch neighbours whose young children established their own stall further down the road from me and closest to traffic coming from Frankston. As a result, all trees were reduced in price over that Christmas as market forces prevailed. Fortunately, they either lost interest awaiting customers or their supply diminished because they did not return the following year. The funniest story about this period of supply and demand was a customer who initially stopped to view my trees late in the afternoon on Christmas Eve, obviously having left it until the last moment to purchase one. I had three trees left but only one was really still in saleable condition, with the others wilting in the summer heat. Dissatisfied with the quality and choice on offer and my price, he opted to try my competitors but soon returned as they had none left.

In the intervening period, a second customer had stopped and expressed an interest in the one saleable tree remaining. Both men became desperate to purchase it and a bidding contest erupted. It eventually sold for the remarkable price of five shillings to the second customer who genuinely did not mind the inflated price. The original customer was so disgruntled that I gave him one of the wilted trees much to his gratitude, and he promised to put it into water as soon as reaching home so it could recover. The true Christmas spirit prevailed that day and everyone was satisfied.

Before our house was eventually constructed, Christmas was celebrated outdoors and naturally, this was where the Christmas tree was erected, subject to weather conditions in summer. If I was asked to recall which Christmas was the best experienced during my early childhood period, it would have been the one when I was around seven or eight years of age. The home was only partially built and we still lived out of the adjacent bungalows that summer, but our huge Christmas tree was inside the incomplete house, albeit partly exposed to the weather. It was adorned with every conceivable decoration, coloured ornaments, baubles, various stars, little plastic trinkets, bells and pine cones sprinkled with glitter hanging from every available branch, sheathed in layers of multi-coloured glittering tinsel, as well as a splattering of smaller presents, cracker Bon-Bons and a delicate angel perched on its tip.

In those days, it was possible to purchase pre-packed Christmas stockings from the larger variety stores ranging in price up to five or ten shillings, depending upon the quality of contents. Each stocking would be crammed with novelties, Bon-Bon crackers, confectionery, comics, colouring books, and small gifts, toys or puzzles for the entire family. These stockings would be hung on the Christmas tree to provide extra flair to the arrangement. Beneath the behemoth tree lay a neatly stacked array of mysterious presents that were expertly camouflaged in beautifully decorative Christmas wrappings stuck together with special red and green festive tape. Every gift was carefully labelled with a small personalised card designating the names of the sender and the receiver to eliminate any confusion.

These gifts remained untouched by prying hands until early on Christmas morning when the entire family gathered and presents distributed in a sen-

Figure 16: Outdoor Christmas tree

sible way. My favourite gift was a cowboy outfit of vest and sturdy fringed leggings known as chaps manufactured from cow hide, complete with a Sheriff's badge and holster for two cap-guns.

I must have worn that outfit for weeks afterwards as it made me feel right at home on the range. Someone else gave me a few boxes containing paper rolls of caps for my toy pistols, which was handy as every cowboy needed ammunition. These small percussion 'caps' made a loud noise when fired

Figure 17: My father the cowboy

simulating a gunshot and generating a puff of smoke for extra realism.

My second favourite present was a box set of realistic building blocks resembling a house from the Olde English Tudor era, with a roof, gables, windows, doors and walls. There certainly was some irony in giving me that gift, given the extended construction status of our own new home.

Who can ever forget the regal Christmas lunch served on a sweltering hot day in summer? In Australia, it was customary to serve piping hot roast meals and warm plum pudding for such tucker, and our family was no exception, even if the outdoor temperature had reached or exceeded the magic mark of 100° Fahrenheit (approaching 38° Celsius). The main course of simmering roast beef or chicken with lashings of every conceivable roasted vegetable and gravy was followed by the magical dessert of all desserts. The homemade plum pudding, complete with various threepenny and sixpenny coins carefully secreted inside and suitably soaked in brandy, was ignited for special effect and then drenched in a brandy custard. For those fortunate enough to score a silver coin in their serving without actually swallowing it, this was an added treat.

At various stages throughout proceedings, a cracker Bon-Bon would be snapped between two of the family by tugging incessantly on either end. Ridiculous or sometimes fancy trinkets, a written joke on a miniscule fragment of paper and coloured tissue-thin hat retrieved from inside the cracker went to the strongest in this contest. I often wondered who compiled these jokes as most were humorous or prophetic, but many were simply too obtuse. The sumptuous lunch and delectable dessert were followed by plates of scrumptious toffees and other confectionery in their individual wrappers, just to complement the festive menu.

If roast chicken had been the main course, there was usually a minor fracas involved to see who ended up with the wishbone from the carcass, and an opportunity for a good luck Christmas wish. This oddly-shaped forked bone known as the furcular was held in the fingers between two members of the family who initially made a wish before snapping it apart. The person retaining the longer piece was believed by tradition to have good fortune or a wish granted, and I suppose the other person got to wash-up the dinner dishes.

All of this delicious repast did nothing towards helping me forget my role in assisting my parents to prepare a chicken for this dinner. First the selected chook had to be caught, involving quite a vigorous chase around the front yard, before being handed over to the executioner. My father usually carried the grim responsibility for this task, much like the operator of the guillotine during the French Revolution in the late 1700s. After the deed, it was again my role to take the bird to my mother for suitable feather-plucking and other cleaning requirements. Fortunately, the executioner's assistant was no longer required from that point, leaving me to resume my daily carefree play activities.

One cannot overlook the most enduring of all airborne pests when living in the bush, and that was the ubiquitous blowfly. No matter what meat or other perishable food source was exposed on a warm day such as Christmas Day, the gigantic blowfly would miraculously appear and land on it. Soon, it was joined by a squadron of like-minded flies wishing to join in the tasting frenzy. The much smaller 'bush flies' sometimes also dominated these raids, but were far less irritating and substantially easier to catch by hand. The solution to control these aerial invasions was by use of the most natural offensive mechanism in the world – the process of swatting a fly.

Most of the family used a rolled-up magazine or newspaper as their preferred instrument of destruction, or even a small commercial fly/bug swatter (meshed small rectangular-shaped flat plastic moulded to a handle), aerodynamically designed to deliver the final splattering blow. Whoever concocted the saying 'that person would not harm a fly' has never been confronted by a barrage of blowflies around food on a hot summer day. I suspect that it may have been the same individual who also proclaimed the common parental warning about every child's indulgence when it came to eating too much confectionery, cakes and ice-cream: 'Your eyes are too big for your belly'.

However, as it was in those days when aerosol fly spray had only just been invented, a suitable equivalent solution of insecticide dispensed through a hand-pumped spray gun was far less gruesome for the blowflies, albeit excellent at spreading the suffocating plume of deadly solution across a room. Nothing quite like that type of flavouring when you were consuming the last of your Christmas plum pudding with custard.

Good Friends and Neighbours

As our Dutch neighbours had originally built their home at the front of their block, they were readily able to access the power transmission lines located along Cranbourne Road, whereas our home at the rear of the block required a separate electrical diversion line across our entire property in order to access mains power. This took years to install at quite some personal expense. These neighbours kept a few pigs on their block and ensured these free range pigs did not escape by electrifying the wire boundary fence between our properties.

Unfortunately, any human touching the fence received quite a wallop from the electric current as well. We had edible, sweet and nutritious blackberries growing along that side of our property, and often picked the berries for jam preserves or for dessert. Blackberry jam spread over a wholemeal slice of toast was exquisite. However, the blackberry plant was also a prickly and invasive weed that grew in dense, almost impenetrable thickets of brambles, making it decidedly difficult to eradicate without spraying chemical herbicides. Even delicately picking those succulent berries by hand became particularly hazardous from the razor-sharp thorns protruding from the plant.

This combination of circumstances created the perfect storm one Sunday afternoon whilst I was collecting the ripe and plump blackberries growing beside the electrified fence. Once I was positioned in the dense thicket of blackberries, every movement had to be cautiously co-ordinated to avoid those deadly thorns scratching me. Even wearing thick protective gloves, a long sleeved shirt and trousers did not prevent the thorns from ripping and tearing my clothing. This was the ultimate obstacle course. Finally with my container full of those prized berries, it was time to carefully extricate myself from the brambles without incurring any further injury.

Then I observed one more generous clump of super large berries growing just out of my reach above the fenceline and foolishly inched forward to remove them, only to receive quite a shock. It was akin to someone suddenly kicking you in the backside with a considerable force.

Despite losing half my harvested berries during the encounter, I still managed to escape major harm both from the fence and the thorns, only to be informed by the neighbour that the plant had been recently sprayed with herbicide to stop it spreading onto his property. All that pain for no gain whatsoever.

We had no immediate neighbours behind our property for many years and it remained undeveloped bushland, but there was a reclusive couple who resided in a rather unique galvanised iron dwelling across on the next unsealed street, well behind our house. The man produced various unusual and sometimes graphic sculptures cut from metal sheeting and hung them from tree branches at the front of his block. Eventually there were no more available trees, so additional sculptures were hung on his balcony or simply affixed to the ground. Inside the dwelling, there were various murals painted on the walls. The couple kept to themselves and were rarely seen around the district. I understood that some local children were scared of the occupants and avoided passing the house wherever possible by using nearby bush tracks instead. I assumed that anyone who was that reclusive and displayed odd artworks about their property might be treated with such caution by youngsters, but I never experienced any concerns about them.

Many of my childhood friends in the 50s lived quite a distance away in the neighbourhood, and over the years, I often spent the entire day at their places, only returning home at dusk. I eventually became quite friendly with at least three other local boys in the district and we tended to undertake quite a few adventures together exploring the local bushland areas and looking for any unusual discoveries. When I was an 11-year-old, two of the boys named Gordon and Gary were nine-year-olds, and the third lad was Gary's brother called Michael and about eight years of age. On one such trek along the back roads of the district that were little more than gravel tracks, we encountered a small abandoned cottage overgrown with vegetation and spent the entire day exploring the disused property. It appeared as if no-one had lived there for years and as if the cottage had been almost entirely swallowed by the surrounding forest.

On another occasion, our group encountered a small swamp with an incredible cluster of ferns and exotic lilies growing wild. We only discovered the marsh at all due to the abundance of frogs that inhabited the waters, and their crescendo of croaking sounds that attracted our attention. The site was nestled in thick shrubby bushland and was virtually invisible from a distance. Birdlife in this swamp was prolific and fascinating; there were even wild ducks nesting nearby. I recall that we encountered a rather large snake that soon sent us homeward-bound.

That pristine swamp had probably never been visited by anyone else, with no obvious signs of any previous human intervention. It made our little group of explorers rather proud of such an unexpected discovery. We should have been far more attentive, because with such prolific birdlife and frogs, there were always going to be predators. This predator was an enormous and lethal copperhead snake that presumably had fed on frogs regularly because it was quite a length. Of all the group foraging through the undergrowth, it had to be Michael the youngest boy at around eight years of age that first spotted its tail. He almost stood on the snake. To describe his reaction as hysterical would be accurate, given the youngster galloped in the opposite direction, brushing everyone else aside in his panic. The snake then disappeared deeper in the swamp, probably more startled than any of us.

When the other boys regained some composure, it was mutually agreed to simply explore another part of the swamp until I provided them with some critical bush knowledge about copperhead snakes. Their preferred habitat is near water, their major diet is frogs, and most importantly, where frogs are common, copperheads congregate in substantial numbers. Imagine several more large snakes lying in wait somewhere else in the undergrowth, and possibly a swamp infested with snakes. This latter thought was too horrible to even contemplate.

We did not investigate further and sensibly beat a hasty retreat towards home, and as far away from snake-heaven as possible. Young Michael led the group withdrawal without the slightest hesitation.

My father only ever took me to the original Langwarrin railway station once in the 1950s in order to take delivery of our new bath tub, but I was always fascinated by its remoteness and small size. It seemed to me that the station was more of a siding platform for freight rather than a thoroughfare suitable for passengers, and I presumed that it was to serve the nearby Military Reserve (now the extensive Langwarrin Flora and Fauna Reserve). An extract describing the rail journey between nearby Baxter and Frankston past this station taken from *Hastings Memories* by Susan Rowe provides an appropriate setting of this landmark:

> … Langwarrin station is surrounded by bush and scrub. The station building is an unmanned corrugated iron shed with a seat in it. It is a short platform with a kerosene lamp that you light (at night) and a red flag (that you display at day) if you want the train to stop. It must have been a big station once, serving the Army Camp. There was a four-track rail yard there, but all the yard tracks have been pulled up. You can still see where the tracks were…[1]

Later research proved me correct. The station was built in 1888 and operated for almost one hundred years until 1981. By 1988, it had been almost entirely removed, with only the platform mound remaining.[2] The extensive history of this rail line was certainly interesting, but the route of the railway to nearby Baxter through dense scrub was far more challenging to a youngster in the 1950s. I suppose that my one and only visit to the Langwarrin railway station some 1.4 miles (2.2 kilometres) from home must have been what motivated me one day to persuade my friends to explore further afield to Baxter railway station, located a further 1.7 miles (2.8 kilometres) away. After all, the journey would be no problem for our band of young but experienced adventurers!

As the same small group of four intrepid and fearless explorers who had previously encountered the snake-swamp, it seemed quite natural for us

Figure 18: Troops Boarding Train at Lang Warren Circa 1916
(© State of Victoria, Public Record Office – State Transport Corporation: Photographic Collection of Railway Negatives, Series VPRS 12800/P1, Item H5151)

to set out from home undaunted around 9 am on this new adventure. Our objective was to trace the rail route on foot to the nearby district of Baxter, a return trek of slightly over six miles (10 kilometres) from home through dense woodlands the entire way. I became the nominated leader of the expeditionary group simply because as an 11-year-old, I had seniority and had actually visited the Langwarrin station. This eventually unfolded into an extraordinarily long day of adventures, mishaps, and becoming lost.

We found untold and interesting numbers of items discarded in the bush, such as automobile parts, tyres, broken furniture, metal sheets, industrial parts, a mattress, disused toys, and even paintings, an old store mannequin and empty suitcases. The challenge however was exacerbated by the typically changeable Melbourne weather of 'four seasons in one day'. The day had begun optimistically enough with fine, sunny and mild conditions, which was why the trek initially seemed a good idea. The weather then deteriorated into passing showers, before becoming fine again briefly, followed by a cold brisk wind and eventually heavy downpours of rain. By late afternoon, foggy conditions prevailed and we became lost yet again. Naturally, none of us had come prepared for the diverse weather, precluding taking sufficient confectionery and soft drink. I recall someone actually brought a banana that was consumed within the first five minutes of our trek. It did not really matter as we continued to trudge through the bush, as long as our lolly supply lasted the journey.

Of the many memorable adventures encountered that day, I recall our group becoming totally lost in the bush at various times and yet it was scarcely a concern. Perhaps it was the innocence of those days and the scarcity of population in the region, but we still managed to reach the Baxter railway station and return safely, simply by using basic bush sense techniques, and having a lot of good luck. Total panic only erupted on a relatively few isolated occasions when all hope of being rescued seemed impossible. The peculiar issue about panic is that it can be extremely contagious, starting with the youngest and most inexperienced of our group before spreading like wildfire to the rest of us.

Having finally reached our destination by mid-afternoon when we sighted Baxter railway station from out of the surrounding dense scrub, much like an oasis of civilisation, any thoughts of a potential rescue immediately evaporated. The youngest explorer, eight-year-old Michael who had often complained about being soaked by the passing showers, scratched by prickly bush and of being cold and hungry, soon forgot his discomfort, assisted by an ample supply of our lollies. A shared sense of exhilaration came over the group that we had successfully negotiated the trek. Why had we been so worried? After all, there was still the remainder of the day to return home and our parents would not become concerned until after 6 pm anyway.

The weather was fine and sunny once more, and after all, we did now know the way home. Then, shortly after re-entering the thick bushland as we trekked homeward, the fickle weather turned misty and eventually foggy. With daylight starting to fade late in the afternoon and the fog becoming almost impenetrable, we fortuitously stumbled across the local railway line again and then a gravel service road. This led us to nearby McClelland Drive, so we opted to remain out of the bushland entirely and quickly followed this connecting road to the major Cranbourne-Frankston Road and almost home in a very short time, and incredibly before the onset of dusk.

It had been an exciting day of discovery and enjoying new places rarely if ever seen driving in a vehicle. I would not have missed that trek for any reason as it had every challenge that a young adventurer enjoyed. I even managed to reach home just before 6 pm and avoid the traditional misfortune of missing my evening meal for being late. That evening, my mother cooked me a generous meal and I pondered how she appreciated that an explorer becomes so hungry being away from home for nine hours? She was not even impressed that my journey had involved reaching Baxter as if it was just around the corner.

Such was the camaraderie of my neighbourhood friends in those days that we mutually decided to band together and collect discarded soft drink bottles to obtain the threepenny (small bottles) or sixpenny (large bottles) refunds payable from shopkeepers. Over almost a year, our group salvaged substantial numbers of empty glass bottles throughout the local district from bushland, roadsides, car parking areas and sporting grounds, and then progressively stockpiled them outside at a friend's house. His father drank beer in large 26 fluid ounce (750 ml) bottles and stored all his empties for the recycling refund from the brewery. It seemed quite a convenient arrangement to have both sets of bottles stored separately in one central location.

As our stockpile had grown significantly, it appeared the opportune time to have them collected for their refund values and share the resultant pocket money. Much like scrap metal dealers, there were people who collected and paid for used glass bottles in bulk: these were subsequently washed and recycled, particularly beer bottles which were very abundant. My friend's father arranged for 'the Bottlo' man to collect the stockpile one weekday afternoon, and after school, we all met at his house to reap our rewards.

My friend greeted us with a very solemn expression and I immediately sensed troubled waters ahead. Although both bottle stockpiles were gone, the Bottlo had only been requested to purchase the beer bottles, but as a favour, opted to take the soft drink bottles away without cost. We received nothing for our diligent recycling efforts and learned quite a confronting lesson concerning financial assets.

Exploring the local district was a full-time hobby for most youngsters, given the widespread extent of pristine bushland in Langwarrin, and the diversity of native wildlife undisturbed by the urban expansion of nearby Frankston. Even Cranbourne was still just a semi-rural community surrounded by orchards and farmlets. Memorable times spent in my travels included the discovery of a long open tract of bushland covered in native grasses that almost resembled the manicured greens of a golf course, exploring sand dunes behind the Langwarrin football ground now known as the Lloyd Park Reserve, and encountering wildlife at very close quarters, such as wallabies, koalas and occasionally, an echidna.

Of course exploratory travels through native bushland around the district also had unexpected hazards from biting insects, particularly enormous red bull ants (*Myrmecia gulosa*) and transient March flies. For anyone who has ever had a bull ant (also known as 'bulldog ants') trapped in their sock and felt the intense sting and resultant excruciating pain, they will know it is almost indescribable. The painful swelling that subsequently develops around the bite(s) is just as bad. Bull ants grow up to an enormous length of 40mm, have characteristic large eyes for superior vision, elongated vice-like mandibles for gripping their prey, and if disturbed around their nest, attack in ferocious swarms that continue to track any intruder for metres. These gigantic ants are well known for their extreme aggressiveness.[3]

I was once stung simultaneously by two of these raiders, one in each sock, and had trouble even walking afterwards for at least 30 minutes. This was because each bull ant can strike multiple times. Their sting is located in their abdomen and injects the victim with a very potent venom while the ant grips onto your flesh with its pincers. It reminded me of another unfortunate encounter with a much smaller — almost miniscule —common black ant when I was quite young around seven or eight-years-old whilst consuming a chocolate biscuit. Unbeknown to me, the poor little insect had taken a quite fancy to chocolate and was on the biscuit as I chewed it. Naturally, it retaliated by biting me on the inside of my mouth.. The enormous and painfully swollen aftermath resulted in me missing a meal or two until I could actually swallow food. I learnt another harsh lesson about nature.

Strangely,a rare encounter with a relatively harmless 15 cm (six inch) long stick insect (*Acrophylla titan*) or phasmid a few years later was the pinnacle of my inglorious history with creepie-crawlies. Stick insects are also known as 'walking sticks, leaf insects, or ghost/apparition insects' due to their natural camouflage resembling sticks, twigs or leaves. Although they supposedly only eat foliage and move incredibly slowly (almost in slow-motion), one of these 'apparitions' miraculously once latched onto to my finger as a child and would not let go. The embarrassment of being bitten by a slow moving stick far outweighed any pain that I incurred.

March flies (*Tabanids*) are stout-bodied horseflies with large eyes, and the female of the species bites mainly animals (and humans) to obtain blood. If one landed on your exposed skin even for a moment, it was swatted instantaneously for fear of their painful bite. It was not uncommon to encounter them on our group adventure travels around swamps and in woodlands in the warmer months, so everyone wore long-sleeved shirts as a precaution. Still, there were usually plenty of bites and you always knew their bite by the sharp pain they inflicted. I suppose explorers have to be tough and these flying predators certainly kept you vigilant at different times of the year when prevailing winds brought them into the district.

The pale yellow sand dunes adjacent to Langwarrin's football ground at Lloyd Reserve were also shared with a nearby operational sand pit, although this was rarely in use over weekends when our exploratory bush excursions occurred. As a consequence, the surrounding land provided relatively unfettered access for our prolific adventures. Many enjoyable hours were spent climbing to the crests of those massive steep dunes and simply tumbling/rolling down their slopes, despite commonly receiving mouthfuls of sand and somewhat sand-riddled hair. We would simply shake it out of our hair and set off to climb the next steeper dune. This all changed into the early 1960s when the sand pit expanded its operations, effectively restricting any public access to the nearby dunes, and we undertook adventures elsewhere.

Langwarrin actually had several operating sand pits scattered around the district as it was part of an expansive inland geological area stretching between Frankston and Cranbourne which comprised a series of large wind-blown (aeolian) dunes and sheets that enveloped the terrain in the last million years.[4] The sands had been so well sorted by wind action that they were evenly graded and free of clay contamination. As a result, such comparatively 'clean' sand was able to be blended with lower quality, coarser clayey sands to successfully produce brick sand.[5]

To some extent, my incredible freedom was also curtailed when I attended primary school, but I still managed to enjoy the wide open spaces on weekends, public holidays and during school term breaks.

Primary School Early Days

Like so many other adult Australians, my parents did not have much opportunity to obtain what most would regard as 'a reasonably acceptable standard of formal education'. Throughout the 1930s, Australia experienced the extreme economic hardships of an era aptly named the Great Depression which commenced in 1929 and lasted until the outbreak of the Second World War in 1939. This unprecedented collapse of financial organisations throughout the industrialised world resulted in substantial and prolonged unemployment, and enforced domestic frugality for most citizens in order to survive. I recall pitiful stories from my father about hundreds of men queuing on the docks in Sydney for a handful of available casual jobs, of large community 'soup-kitchens' erected in the city to feed the homeless each day, and of many families often routinely going without many of the basic necessities of life. Formal education rated very poorly on the social scale in those impoverished times.

The Second World War (1939 -1945) resulted in further financial restrictions on family life as Australians focused on supporting the war effort. Living standards remained low as families continued to experience shortages of essential commodities and menfolk went overseas to join the war. By the 1950s as Australia entered a new transformation period of major economic and population growth, expectations about educational requirements also changed drastically. Parents no longer accepted that schooling was optional for their children, or that 'getting work was more important than receiving an education'.

Governments and communities alike recognised that new generations of better educated children were essential to support the burgeoning industrial growth underway across the nation, and so primary school education changed to ensure the best possible outcomes for Australia's children. The change was relatively conservative and the results virtually unnoticeable until the early 1960s, but the expectations of parents were quite apparent – that each and every child deserved to receive an education and schooling was compulsory for all. Most children wanted to attend school and their parents agreed.

Langwarrin Primary School No.3531 which I attended between 1956 and 1962 was a relatively modest educational institution in the local shire district of Cranbourne, and located on a rise over 220 yards (200 metres) along Warrandyte Road from the main road linking Cranbourne to Frankston. It was housed in a relatively old weatherboard building located on a small property of about 2 acres (0.8 hectares) and comprised three classrooms for beginners and junior pupils (5-7 years of age), intermediate level (8-9 years of age) and senior pupils (10-12 years of age), as well as a staff room

Figure 19: Original Langwarrin North State School in 1915

(Victorian Education Department, Reproduced from ' Langwarrin, 100 Years of Schooling 1890-1990')

and ablutions. The layout of the property was well-planned, with a grassed oval at the back of the block for sporting activities, and an adjacent sand pit play area for the youngest pupils. At the front of the property, there was a hard-surfaced quadrangle assembly area, an asphalt netball court and nearby maypole, shelter shed and miscellaneous storage sheds for garden tools and firewood.

Langwarrin Primary School No.3531 had commenced on 1st January 1907 in a temporary class room rented in the Methodist Church located at the opposite end of the local district to its final site. By 1913, a new school had been built at its Warrandyte Road site, comprising a single room with 30 pupils enrolled and known as 'Langwarrin North' State School.[1]

A second room was added in 1932 and by early 1950, the third classroom and a staff room completed the school which had an enrolment of 79 by that time. In June 1955, the 'North' was dropped from the school name and it assumed the title of Langwarrin's only primary school.[2] There were originally two other schools in the overall broader district with this place title and subsequently renamed: Langwarrin School No. 2961 in 1889 (subsequently Pearcedale School by 1908) and Langwarrin Station Railway School No.3023 in 1890 (eventually Baxter School by 1919).[3]

In 1955, there was no kindergarten, day care facility or other equivalent child-minding service (apart from grandparents of course). There was bubs' grade for those children just about ready for primary school but not quite. The pre-condition applicable for attending bubs' grade was neatly combed hair, clean and ironed clothing, and most importantly, an immaculately spotless handkerchief. There would be trouble if you neglected to bring a handkerchief and inspections could be convened at short notice. Then there was the delightful Miss Smith who taught first and second graders as well as the beginners in bubs' grade. I recall her as a very special young woman with a great love of children, who displayed considerable patience and kindness throughout her teaching endeavours.

In this rather unusual world of first-time schooling, Plasticine and coloured paper of various sheet sizes and shades ruled supreme. The choice of colours and tones was immense with every conceivable shade of the rainbow as well as brown, grey and black. We enjoyed unlimited access to crayons, coloured chalk and more coloured paper for all those fiddly works. Cutting paper using small safety scissors and then pasting with Clag paste was a very popular pastime in this grade, as was scribbling on writing slates with coloured chalk. The wonder of Clag adhesive paste was that the original composition was starch-based, and thus easily washed off, non-staining and non-toxic. It was white and sticky when applying, yet dried to a clear finish in only 10-20 minutes. The product came in small 10 ounce net weight (283 grams) glass bottles complete with a convenient brush applicator.

What an idyllic life for a five-year-old who had left home for the first time to spend several hours with complete strangers called 'teachers'. Normally I would have brought my furry teddy ('Ted') for company, but now I was a big boy and could do it all alone. What was I worried about in bubs' grade? There were others like me but they all brought their dolls and furry toys. Somehow, I just intuitively knew that I would enjoy school and Miss Smith and all that coloured paper and glue for free. How soon before we could start using lead and coloured pencils?

By first and second grade, the shelter shed where pupils spent morning recess and lunch breaks, and sheltered from passing inclement weather, was to figure prominently in my school life. Comparing each other's sandwich fillings and fruit in each lunch box was mandatory between classmates until Peter Poulson arrived. What made him so different to the rest of us? Peter had expensive Pascall's Fruit Bon Bons in his lunch box most days – 'hard on the outside but sensationally soft on the inside'. Each Bon Bon was individually wrapped and tasted exquisitely like real fruit such as strawberry, pineapple, raspberry or blackcurrant. They are still manufactured today. His sandwich fillings were fresh ham and homemade pickles, premium corned beef or some other expensive delight. Sometimes he also had a rich pastry or cake. The rest of us usually had boring cheese and tomato, cheese and salad or simply tomato sandwiches, plus an apple or pear. If I wanted a dessert such as cake, it was purchased from the corner tuck shop using my meagre pocket money. Unfortunately for Peter, he often failed the infamous 'clean handkerchief inspection test' on many mornings at school, and he never ever offered his lollies to anyone else. Odd what you recollect about some people after all that time.

The rest of those early years in first and second grade was really about enjoying myself. I still recollect the asphalt netball court used at lunch breaks for various scurrilous team games like British bulldog, fish in the net, and other equally injurious games. Many scratches and bruises were incurred from those 'rough and tumble' play games. The school's maypole usually got quite a work-out at recess breaks, if you were able to reach the metal grip rings. For those not acquainted with a maypole, it was a tall cylindrical pole with a series of loose chains of equal length affixed to its upper end in a rotating carousel, permitting each chain in turn to rotate freely around the pole.

At the other end of each length of chain was a sturdy iron metal ring for gripping and pulling the chain around the pole. By running and swinging on each chain, the carousel would be forced to swivel around the top of the pole. For the younger children who barely reached the grip rings, it meant hanging on grimly whilst stronger older children ran and swung on their respective chains. Woe betide those who hung on too long and were flung off in sudden flight to land outside the sandy safety pit.

The introduction of a maypole as a standard item of play equipment in the primary school was to promote exercise, strengthen all the muscles and actively improve childhood health to assist with the growing process. It was a clever strategy by teachers of combining exercising the body with children's play activities in a thoroughly enjoyable way, unless you were flung off the maypole.

My other vivid memory about those earliest years of school was the daily tradition of singing our National Anthem, entitled 'God Save the Queen'. Even at my young age, it became mandatory to know the words and usually sing them with fervour to indicate our allegiance to both Queen and Country. The Queen and the Nation as an integral part of the British Empire (eventually becoming the British Commonwealth) were very important to education, as it was an all-British traditional education system. Another tradition learnt in those early days was how to bow politely when acknowledging an official dignitary visiting our school.

Figure 20: The Giant Stride 1911

(Woods Hutchinson, *A Handbook of Health*)

It had to be … just a neat bow, feet together, bend from the waist in a snappy, no-nonsense doubling up, right arm across the stomach, left arm across the back. Quick and neat. For a girl, it was far more involved and was called curtseying. Left foot behind right foot, knees bent together making sure they didn't lock, hold out the skirt (even … if wearing shorts and plastic sandals and blouses), incline the head graciously, and count: one two down, three four up.[4]

The daily inspection routine by the teacher for the cleanliness of young pupils in first and second grades upon their arrival at class continued unabated from the earlier bubs' grade. Were your shoes polished and laces tied correctly? Did you have clean fingernails and was your hair neatly combed (boys) or brushed (girls)? It was not uncommon for the proverbial note to be sent home with you for your parents if these misdemeanours continued. The dreaded note in a sealed envelope was always to be feared, and yet had to be delivered by the offending pupil as the ill-fated messenger.

Then I entered the intermediate years of my schooling when learning became much more focused on crucial life skills. My school teacher was Mrs Adderly.

Although Mrs Adderly was born in England, I understand that she possibly spent almost her entire teaching life at this school, commencing not long after 1913. She married into a family in 1926 who had been associated with the Langwarrin district since the early 1900s and her husband had started one of district's general stores (*Arcadia*) in the 1950s. She resided in a stylish but unusual cottage known as *Mossbank* not far from school, set back from Cranbourne Road on a circular driveway. It had the exterior façade of a stately Tudor residence complete with clinker bricks and a steeply pitched roof.[5] Surprisingly to me, it also resembled the sugar candy confectionery cottage from the well-known Germanic fairy tale *Hansel and Gretel* by the Brothers Grimm. I did not easily recollect this teacher's first name (it was actually Ida) as we only addressed her as Mrs Adderly at all times. I do recall her strict punitive measures for those not conforming to the rigid standards and protocols of primary school education in the late 50s.

Amongst third and fourth graders, Mrs Adderly had quite a reputation for ruling her classes with an iron fist, although she was a very experienced teacher nonetheless. Justice would be dispensed to any unfortunates in a swift and most decisive manner, usually involving a ruler and some resultant sore knuckles. There would be no ambiguity regarding her intent whatsoever. The pupil needed to focus on the scholastic tasks being taught and not behave as a miscreant. Mrs Adderly was at this point a portly bespectacled woman in her early sixties, with a forthright personality and quite a daunting appearance to mere third and fourth graders. She commanded respect on sight. As a result, we tended to listen intently and work diligently without resorting to the idle chatter or foolish pranks to which some young children were prone.

In hindsight, I perceived that she had far more positive outcomes on me than I ever imagined in those tender youthful years. She taught me the sense of purpose and self-discipline needed to learn effectively by listening rather than by chattering. She endowed me with the motivation to learn more about education. In a broader sense, I also learnt the mechanics of considerable lifelong skills of the 3R's – reading, (w)riting and (a)rithmetic which continue to serve me well today.

Who can ever forget indelibly memorising the multiplication tables, thus being readily able to multiply difficult combinations such as 7 x 9 or 11 x 12 instantaneously? Above all else, she instilled in me a respect for those who knew far more than me and who were willing to share their knowledge freely in a productive way. Nothing wrong with a tad of strict discipline to keep us on the right track to learning. In the modern era, such disciplinary actions would probably be viewed as brutal and unnecessary, but times were vastly different in that golden era, as in the following account:

> They taught you the way you should be educated … your reading, your writing, your arithmetic … They dwelt on that. And if you didn't know your timetables [multiplication tables], "Hand out!" Strap. "Ow!" No, they were quite strict on making sure that later on in life you knew how to add up and how to talk.[6]

I understand that Mrs Adderly eventually retired in 1962 which was my last year of primary schooling, and now realise how fortunate I was being taught for two years by this amazing and diligent teacher.

It was at this time of my schooling in third and fourth grades that I was introduced to using nib pens, blotting paper and inkwells in one-seater desks. I had only previously used HB lead pencils, colouring pencils, crayons and chalk, while sitting around small tables with other children of six to seven years of age. Now it was time to become familiar with the writing instruments essential in later adult life and be assigned a proper desk. Only the relatively wealthy could afford ink fountain pens either to own as a status symbol or to give as a present to others. The icon of all fountain pens was the Parker pen that was promoted as 'the most perfect pen in the world' due to its unique Aero-metric Ink System for scientifically storing and delivering the ink. It always sounded like something from the Space Age and had an expensive price to match, particularly if you had to replace the fountain pen's nib.

The ubiquitous, inexpensive and disposable ballpoint pen known as a Biro which would eventually revolutionise writing, had yet to enter the Australian education system. This left only one choice for pupils.

A nib pen was truly an artisan's writing tool – it was dipped gingerly into a small inkwell containing either black, blue or red Indian (India) ink, excess gently shaken from the sharp nib's point and the writing process commenced. For a right-handed person, it was incredibly easy to write as the hand progressed away from the inked words. For a left-handed person like me, the writing hand smudged those words unless meticulously dried with blotting paper. This highly absorbent paper came in standard sheets and effectively soaked up the excess liquid ink of written words, making it invaluable to us left-handers. Eventually, I taught myself to write like a right-handed person with my left hand, so removing the unnecessary need for continuous blotting. This pen was inexpensive and rarely required a replacement nib unless its tip had been blunted – it was an affordable writing implement for pupils.

The following commentary on the dilemma of being left handed recalled by a primary school pupil named Donald Stock in rural South Australia between 1948 and 1955 has remarkable similarities to my humble circumstances:

> … I used to have strife when I was young because I was left handed and you're supposed to do heavy down-strokes and light up-strokes when you're writing – I couldn't get on with the nibs – I used to dig them into the paper all the time and flick ink everywhere – I was always in strife and having ink splattered all

over the page ...[7]

Desk inkwells routinely required daily replenishment of their ink supply, as these small porcelain containers only held very limited quantities, soon consumed by writing. For the unfortunate boys selected at random to be ink monitors, it meant daily cleaning and replenishment of the class inkwells, with the occasional catastrophic spillage of ink when overfilling an inkwell. I can only assume girls were not selected for this arduous task due to the impact of having wet Indian ink staining their hands after such incidents. This ink was incredibly difficult to remove even after washing with a bar of the wonderful Solvol soap. If ever there was a better heavy duty pumice soap for removing tough ingrained dirt, oily grease, paint, ink and solvents, it had yet to be invented. Whenever my mother threatened to wash-out my mouth after hearing unsavoury language, I always prayed that it would not be using 'that soap' which could remove far more than just my nasty words.

Writing in those days was mostly artistic and fluid in style rather than strictly rigid. The pen was a mighty instrument, but the nib pen was sometimes randomly used by some naughty characters in the class rather like a spear, which could be a painful experience for anyone on the receiving end. I also understand that the dipping of a girl's pigtails into an inkwell from the desk behind was not an uncommon practice. Teachers spent considerable time writing on a massive blackboard located in each classroom using white and coloured chalk, and pupils were expected to diligently copy much of the information into their exercise books. The process provided structure to each lesson and copying the information reinforced the crucial elements of the learning process.

Perhaps the most memorable event to occur in those intermediate school grades was the infamous case of the pocket money thief. Our school building had one central interior corridor from which the three major classrooms were entered. An extended row of hooks was affixed along each wall of this corridor for pupils to hang their coats, hats and carry bags containing their morning recess snack and lunches. The apparel and bags hung on these hooks were left unattended all day without any incident over many years, such was the honesty and integrity of the pupils. Then, mysteriously, pocket money started to disappear from miscellaneous bags. Only a few coins were taken initially from select bags and went relatively unnoticed, until eventually many children complained of losing all of their pocket money. This could mean no money available to purchase lunch or perhaps after-school treats on the way home, and quite a despicable act for those days.

The culprit was ultimately caught red-handed in the heinous act by a teacher. The girl, who was from the fifth or sixth grade, was originally from England. By coincidence, I was a close friend of her younger brother who regularly played soccer with me at school. Total humiliation was to follow for this poor misguided girl who was made to stand in front of the entire school assembly early one morning and apologise profusely to make amends for her crime. To exhibit sincere remorse in front of her fellow classmates was an adequate punishment and certainly sent a powerful message of contrition. This petty crime only ever happened once in my time at primary school, but was never forgotten by me.

On the sensitive subject of school discipline, 1950s punishment meted out to offenders always matched the offence. At the lowest end of the punitive scale for a pupil was being sent to pick up every scrap of waste paper and other miscellaneous litter around the entire school premises. If the offender committed a slightly more serious transgression, it was writing a prescribed sentence repetitively somewhere between 10 and 100 times, and delivering it to the teacher the following day. School detention after class was rare indeed. For the most odious offences, perhaps being caught smoking behind the wood shed, striking another pupil, or repeated mischief, it was corporal punishment known as the dreaded rattan cane or 'the cuts'. This was not to be confused with the less severe hand ruler that any teacher could freely use on-the-spot to discipline pupils across their knuckles for daily infractions, such as compulsive chatting or other minor misbehaviour in class. They both hurt momentarily.

The only punishment worse than the physical pain of being caned was the ordeal of facing the headmaster who wielded the archaic weapon. He kept it securely stored in the 'Big Room' – the room used for teaching the fifth and sixth grade classes. The unfortunate miscreant stood in front of the fifth and sixth graders in this room with an open hand extended awaiting their just desserts. If the pupil was lucky, it might only be one cursory swipe with the cane, if not, it could be a few times. Any miscreant withdrawing their hand before the cane struck only incurred further punishment. Although it never happened to me, I understand from others that the embarrassment of being punished by the headmaster far outweighed any short term pain experienced from receiving 'the cuts'. In hindsight, although corporal punishment was abolished in public schools throughout most of Australia (excluding the Northern Territory) in the 1980s and 1990s, it still served a useful disciplinary purpose in the golden era, possibly due to its effectiveness as a potential deterrent. Everyone feared corporal punishment, and as a result, canings were very rare in our school.

This period of my life was my first introduction to dental health care and the misfortunes reaped from consuming excessive confectionery. When I was very young, the only dental issues involved the nocturnal visit of the 'Tooth Fairy'. As my baby teeth fell out from time to time, each tooth was carefully concealed beneath my pillow overnight and in the morning, the tooth would be gone, replaced with a silver sixpence. I never did see the mysterious tooth fairy at work but thoroughly enjoyed the reliable custom of increasing my pocket money. As I grew older, all those tempting sugary sweets, delicious ice creams and fizzy soft drinks that children enjoy came at quite some personal cost.

The two dreaded dental words that most children feared above all else were 'tooth cavities', and this condition was certainly outside of the expertise of the Tooth Fairy. It conjured mental images of unbearable aching mouth pain even before reaching the dentist. Worse still, it probably meant another terrible word might be heard, and that of 'extraction'. More pain and torment was unavoidable once it was necessary to use a very sharp needle to apply anaesthetic for nullifying the original pain. As an eight or nine-year-old, a simple visit to the dentist for me represented a prolonged excursion taking the entire day.

The journey commenced with a 30 minute early morning bus trip between home and the Frankston railway station, and a further 60 minute train trip into Melbourne. As I rarely travelled on electric trains in my childhood days, this part of the journey was very enlightening. In those bygone days before there was any public awareness of the health risk of personal exposure to secondary cigarette smoke, Metropolitan trains comprised six carriages for smokers and one carriage designated for non-smokers. If this sole carriage was already full to capacity, non-smokers had to share the remaining carriages with a cloud of exhaled smoke or await the next train. Even opening the carriage windows rarely improved the interior smoke-filled environment. Fortunately commencing our journey at the start of the Frankston-Melbourne train line meant that we easily found seats in the non-smoking carriage. This was not always the case on the return journey when the train was already packed with passengers.

Figure 21: Flinders Street railway station

After arriving in the city at Flinders Street railway station, there was a 30 minute combined walk and electric tram ride almost to the top end of Spring Street. The Melbourne Dental Hospital, as it was known in the 50s until renamed in 1969, was located just opposite nearby Nicholson Street where it joined Spring Street. Consequently, trams would deviate along their tracks to swing into this street when departing Spring Street, yielding excessive squealing and clanking sounds as their metal wheels crossed over other tramlines. This clearly audible noise was irritating when the hospital windows were open in the upstairs dental rooms, but had the benefit of masking any painful yelps or cries from patients experiencing their remedial dentistry.

Waiting for my turn to be treated required sitting quietly on a wooden bench directly outside the dental rooms, and so unavoidably hearing other patients inside as they were being treated. This did not calm my nerves in the slightest. Then it was my turn for the dentist's chair. In those days, large stainless steel needles were used applying anaesthetic into facial gums and as they became progressively blunt, would be resharpened. Sometimes such needles in need of resharpening took a few unsuccessful attempts before being effective, and that really hurt.

Finally, the process of adding a new tooth filling or the more painful extraction of a tooth was underway. It was not the high pitched whining of the dentist's drill in my ears that was so distressing, but rather my anticipation of the drill inadvertently striking a nerve. Extractions involved much tugging and twisting with surgical pliers to remove a tooth. The physical wrestling involved was more disconcerting than painful, and then it was finally all over. What had I been so concerned about after all? If only the mythical Tooth Fairy could have performed overnight dental work, then all this prolonged travel and intense trepidation would have been avoided.

As my mother usually took me to the iconic old Coles Cafeteria in Melbourne's Bourke Street for lunch afterwards, it greatly relieved my nervous tension. Unfortunately, my face was generally still numb from the procedure, meaning eating or drinking was impossible without drooling or dribbling my food. On other occasions, when I had simply had a non-invasive check-up, eating at this landmark cafeteria was paradise.

It was located on the first floor of a multi-storey building in the heart of the busy city and occupied the entire floor level. The cafeteria was promoted as a family restaurant and designed on a grand scale to accommodate more than 1000 people who were squeezed into a sea of small Laminex dining tables throughout the floor. It became so popular for lunch in Melbourne that we often had to patiently wait for other customers to vacate a table before rushing to occupy their chairs. Once we had temporarily reserved a dining table, it was off to select our lunch by each taking an aluminium food tray and joining the endless queue that flowed past the various food-dispensing stations located around each wall, and there were many.

The choice of quality food of offer was extensive, with every conceivable hot and cold meal, flavoursome snacks, desserts and liquid refreshments readily available for purchase. Menus listed culinary fare from lamb, beef and chicken roasts with vegetables to fish, steaks, chops and stews, from fruit pies, cakes and slices to ice creams, whipped cream delights and jelly, as well as fruit juices, cordials, milk, tea and coffee. Just when you decided that you had chosen correctly, the moving queue took you past more selections and more purchases. Most of the enjoyment of this lunch was in trying to finally decide on those diverse choices. Even basic staples like sandwiches were made from various breads and with a vast range of fillings.

I still believe to this day that sandwiches of soft curried egg cut into quarters were the only edible food for someone who had just undergone tooth fillings or extractions, and still remain my favourite selection today. Finally, we reached the check-out counter, paid for our selections and staggered under the weight of our overloaded food trays back to our 'reserved table' only to find it already occupied. To avoid any disagreement with those already seated, we withdrew discreetly to avoid a fight with the occupiers, and desperately sought any vacant table before settling in to consume the feast. All too soon, lunch was over and it was time to catch a train back home and return to school the next morning, regardless of my dental procedure.

I can only reinforce that going into hospital appeared far worse to me than a visit to the dreaded dentist, and fortunately I missed out on that experience, unlike my siblings. From their graphic accounts, hospitals were places where parental visits were brief and severely restricted to prescribed times of day. From a child's perspective, the wards appeared austere, cold and very sterile with a dominant pungent aroma of antiseptic. Even the bedding was uncomfortably hygienic and the mattresses almost rigid. Even if they had been exaggerating these experiences just to scare me, I had no incentive to go to hospital as a youngster, let alone stay in one.

The Senior Years

By the start of 1961 when I was 10 years of age, it was time to graduate into the fifth and sixth graders' room, ominously named the 'Big Room'. Only the school's headmaster taught in this room. Mr John (Joe) Caulfield was the headmaster in my last year at Langwarrin in 1962: a bespectacled decorated veteran of the Second World War with a broken nose, and a distinctive physical appearance who had lived quite a life before his teaching career. He would sometimes stand at one of the windows and briefly reminisce about his past war experiences as an integral part of our broader education, and it certainly provided a real-life exposure to such matters for us all. Even more surprising was when an old rusted machine gun still mounted on a tripod was found stored in the school's garden shed and resurrected for an upcoming ANZAC day ceremony. Amazing the historical significance of finding such an artefact of warfare.

Becoming a senior pupil in the Big Room meant increased responsibilities for me, and I was awarded the privilege of becoming the school's sole milk monitor. In 1950, the Commonwealth Government introduced a centralised public health scheme to provide all school-age children under the age of thirteen in Australia with free fresh milk supplied daily on weekdays in one third pint glass bottles. The primary purpose of the scheme was to ensure such children received their recommended daily intake of calcium: something that did not appear to be occurring in post-war Australia. The scheme would last over 20 years until 1973 before being ultimately scrapped after providing an entire generation with free milk.[1]

As the milk monitor, it was my role to ensure the small milk bottles delivered in crates to the school entrance gate around 9 am each morning were distributed to each pupil, and to return all empty bottles for recycling the following day. There were only two minor problems with this system. Firstly, there was no refrigeration on school premises to keep the milk cool in summer months until consumed at the 10.30 am morning recess. Not much that I could do about that situation. Secondly, there was the issue of what to do with excess milk remaining when pupils were absent from school. My innovative solution was to consume the excess unwanted milk myself. In those bygone days, the fresh milk was full cream with a thick layer sitting atop of each bottle. On hot summer mornings, the warm milk and cream layer would not necessarily be a good combination if left out in the sun. Suffice to say, unused milk bottles would remain intact on some days and be returned unopened for good reason.

Being now in the fifth grade at Langwarrin Primary meant much more emphasis on sporting opportunities. Mr Ron Lipman was the school's physical education teacher and I owe him a gratitude of thanks for his encouragement of all students to participate in a diversity of sports, including softball, football, soccer, cricket, netball and various athletic endeavours. The school's small grassy oval at the rear of the property was ideal for athletics training, various ball sports and other healthy outdoor activities.

Each year our primary school would participate in the annual Eastern Peninsula District School Sports involving at least one dozen other schools from neighbouring districts and considerably further afield. It would be a major day on the school calendar when all the pupils would travel by coach to a substantial sports ground at Hastings opposite Western Port Bay slightly over 9 miles away (15 kilometres), gaily singing various Australiana outback songs in perfect harmony and unison. Each school's contestants would parade around this enormous ground to loud marching music blaring from amplifiers, creating a tremendous atmosphere and feel to the special day.

The day involved predominantly running and jumping events (including the notorious sack races in heavy duty jute potato bags) of every imaginable type in the morning, followed by many team events in the afternoon to complete the program. For those individuals fortunate enough to win or place consistently in their own age groups, the reward was a magnificent royal blue silk sash embroidered with regal gold lace. For the senior pupils, this meant becoming the champion girl and boy for the entire Peninsula region.

Figure 22: Langwarrin State School Athletics Team

(Ron Daley, Frankston Standard, 18 April 1962 Issue)

I was fortunate to eventually win this premier award in sixth grade in 1962 after just falling short and finishing second in the previous year. The championship sprint over 100 yards was usually the decider and pitted you against seven of the best runners from other schools. It was a standing start (not crouching on starting blocks) in either flat-sole sandshoes or in bare feet (not wearing sprinter's spikes). I still remember that sprint lucidly today and how close the finish was between myself and another competitor, with millimetres to spare. Such races were almost like it would have been in ancient Greece during the original Olympics, based upon pure ability alone. Our school also won the C.H.Hodgins Shield for Athletic Skill that year, which I shared with Langwarrin's senior girl Susan Eddy.

Figure 23: Individual champions

(Ron Daley, Frankston Standard, 18 April 1962 Issue)

Figure 24: Langwarrin School Captains

(Ron Daley, Frankston Standard, 18 April 1962 Issue)

Susan was a very versatile young lady who could match it with anybody. Independently-minded, tough by nature and a great friend, she always wore her long hair in plaits and (as I recollect) preferred jeans or shorts to wearing a skirt. Nobody was able to beat her in the girls' events at Langwarrin due to her sheer determination in winning. Having her as a friend was definitely to my benefit. On one occasion, we had a playful wrestle on the way home from school as you do when you are young, and she beat me easily. Susan's resolve and stamina made me glad that she was on our team at the sports carnival.

Two of my most memorable team events at the annual Eastern Peninsula District School Sports were tunnel ball and the relay, and further elaboration is definitely needed to fully appreciate how difficult these events were to complete successfully. Team selection was critical to success as the relay required four of the school's fastest junior or senior sprinters, depending upon the age group. Conversely, tunnel ball teams relied upon both speed and dexterity skills across several pupils.

Tunnel ball rules required each team to form a straight line facing in the same direction with their legs standing apart to make a tunnel. The last team member at the end of the line stood with their knees bent and head down awaiting the ball's arrival through this tunnel of legs. Only the team member at the front of the line who initially held the basketball/netball stood at a fixed spot facing towards the line of participants in the opposite direction. When the event started, this team member quickly rolled the ball into the tunnel, and each of the participants progressively assisted its passage until it reached the end of the tunnel. The last team member caught the ball, sprinted to the original fixed spot at the head of line and repeated the process of rolling the ball, before rejoining the tunnel line after the ball had reached the end. As this happened, the entire line of participants shuffled slightly backwards one position to permit the person carrying the ball to rejoin the tunnel.

When all participants had completed their turns, the final team member then sprinted with the ball to a finish line located well past the head of the line. Only the fastest team to complete the event with the ball was victorious. It may not sound complicated but this sport was fraught with disasters. The most common mistake was rolling the ball too quickly or violently so that it struck one of the participant's legs, causing the ball to deviate out of the tunnel. The offending team member then had to retrieve the ball and resume its passage along the tunnel, consuming valuable time. The most comical mistake was when the team member at the end of the line actually let the ball pass through their legs instead of trapping it. Imagine a ball whizzing along the tunnel of legs and propelled by many hands in the line, only to go straight past the last participant at speed. A fast pursuit ensued to gather the ball located probably 20 to 30 yards away.

Combine this situation with two adjacent tunnel ball teams making the same mistake at the same time, and the balls becoming mixed up. Did I retrieve the right ball just because it was closer or would our team be disqualified for cheating? I recall one team at those sports being unable to even complete the passage of the ball through the tunnel of legs without it constantly deviating away into the distance. All other teams had finished and this unfortunate group was still only about halfway through the event.

The relay was certainly not as complex but required precision and extreme speed. In those days, the team relay was held over four identical stages and required the participants to simply sprint about 75-100 yards (about 70-90 metres) from one end of the sports ground to the other, and pass the relay baton to a stationary team member who then sprinted back over the same path. With your outstretched arm awaiting the incoming baton, you waited anxiously, standing carefully behind the start line. Imagine someone approaching you at considerable speed, handing over the precious relay baton, only for you to drop it. As the competitors sprinted away with their batons, you would have to make up lost ground as a result over an incredibly short distance. Fortunately for me, I was often selected to be the last runner in the relay team and managed to win my leg due to my sprinting prowess, as long as I did not drop the dreaded baton. I still believe to this day that sprinting from a standing start wearing only flat-soled sandshoes or no footwear at all had to be the hardest way to win an athletics event, even as a youngster.

On the bus journey back to our school after the end of a most successful day's athletics, the chorus of voices merrily singing more Australiana songs was almost deafening, yet thoroughly enjoyable. Even the teachers joined in the revelry of the songs *The Happy Wanderer* or *Along the Road to Gundagai*, and some were not bad singers at all.

Folk dancing was a very popular pastime in the early 60s for the pupils at primary school. By my final year in the sixth grade, I had managed to perfect many of the closely synchronised dance steps of various exotic tunes from overseas with my English dancing partner Eileen Cooper. When I reminisce about those days, it is quite astonishing that as young people, we were so adept at formal dancing. Perhaps the choices of entertainment were not as diverse as they are these days, and so we made the most of our available options. I recall one day in the sixth grade performing a demonstration folk dance with Eileen Cooper in front of the entire school assembly. I surmise that those days of entertainment are now long gone from primary school education, which is unfortunate given the intricate skills involved.

Folk dancing probably sounds boring and outdated by today's standards, but at least it was not square dancing that was extremely popular in Australia by the beginning of the 1950s. It became a community craze throughout the country even to the extent of conducting National Championships. I suppose having a caller in front of the square dancers loudly reciting the sequential steps to the music helped considerably as well. Fortunately by the time I was old enough to dance, the craze had well and truly passed. The following tongue-in-cheek commentary from someone who recalled the craze perhaps says much about that period to me:

> … From what I remember, for a man, you needed a weak mind, a check shirt, stupid heavy boots, a wide belt with big buckle, sometimes a broad-brimmed hat, and uncomfortable stiff pants like blue jeans. The girls also needed a weak mind, wide multi-coloured skirts, pretty white blouses, and something like bobby sox. If you had these, you could swing your partner to the left, and dosado to your heart's content.[2]

Another interesting pupil at Langwarrin Primary School was Olive Carter who had the enviable advantage of living directly adjacent to the school premises. At lunch breaks, she would stroll out of the entrance gate and one minute later, would be home. It gave an entirely new meaning to be called a local. Running late for school as have slept in one morning? Sixty seconds later, and you were in class. However, I always felt incredibly sorry for Olive, given her home's proximity to school. Give me the wide open spaces any day.

The wood shed at school warrants a special mention at this time. By sixth grade, we were deemed responsible enough to sensibly and safely chop the timber mill offcuts and forest wood blocks for the school's combustible heaters in those bitter cold Victorian winters, as you did in semi-rural schools then. Unfortunately, the wood shed also provided suitable camouflaged cover for those rogue pupils electing to smoke cigarettes, even at the prime age of 12-years-old. Smoking amongst the older pupils was still seen as trendy and even hip, particularly if you borrowed your smokes from your relatives. As they would probably discover in much later life, it can be a very short life indeed,

The Big Room only ever experienced a criminal break-in once in my time at school when someone forced open a sliding window to gain entry one night, but left clues everywhere inside the building, including various dead matches scattered across the floor. Obviously the intruder(s) went looking in the dark for anything of value and took nothing because the supply of matches ran out. Bright sparks can certainly generate dumb ideas.

One of the distinct advantages of sixth grade was that it was a preparation for secondary schooling in the following year. Sixth graders were the seniors of the primary school and as a consequence, were provided with more responsibilities and of course, quite a latitude of scholastic freedom. In 1962, we were sent on a rare excursion outside of the district to the local Frankston soft drink factory operated by Peninsula Cordials to learn more about the commercial world of manufacturing. It was a time when only glass bottles of soft drink were being manufactured, and stored in wooden crates for distribution. For some of us in the group, it was also an ideal time to savour every conceivable flavour of aerated water – pineapple, orange, lemon, lime, kola, creamy soda, raspberry, and lemonade. As part of the detailed inspection process of every stage of the operation, we all went away having consumed more than ample stocks of fizzy drink, which in hindsight was indeed a rare visit for any child. Such an opportunity was not to be missed.

I understand that Langwarrin's old weatherboard school eventually outgrew its educational usefulness with an escalating pupil enrolment and an increasing reliance on several transportable classrooms and public facilities. By 1969, the School President described the old school '…as being possum and rat infested and having inadequate toilet facilities'. A new school opened on a substantially larger site on the opposite side of Warrandyte Road in mid-1970 with over 200 children and eight classrooms.[3] The original block of land was heavily planted with trees by the school with the intent to turn it into an arboretum and bird sanctuary, and I hope that they succeeded as there were too many memories on that site to forget. In 2005, it was sold by the Education Department.[4] The end of a historical era of primary schooling had arrived.

I thoroughly enjoyed all of my primary schooling years at Langwarrin, but if I had to nominate some very special memories, then it would be of the local Tuck Shop located on the corner of Warrandyte and Cranbourne Roads, my interesting school friends from that era, and the many childhood adventures experienced when travelling between home and school.

The Corner Tuck Shop and Friends

The local Tuck Shop was actually an Ampol petrol station and service bay with a shop attached for selling a very diverse range of goods. In those bygone days, an attendant would dispense the petrol, check the engine oil and clean the car's windscreens, whereas nowadays, all these transactions have become strictly self-service. However, this was no ordinary service station and convenience shop. It was almost akin to a combination grocery store, delicatessen, confectionery emporium and vehicle spare parts outlet. An apt description of this unique facility is provided:

> … they cleared the bush block on the corner of Warrandyte Road and Cranbourne Road…and built a small convenience store and garage…This store had petrol, some groceries, a milk bar with ice creams, a couple of tables and chairs where people could sit and have a cup of tea, and was also the tuck shop for the school. They also sold all sorts of odds and ends and soft toys made by a local lady…[1]

The choice of confectionery in this shop was overwhelming and could change from week to week. You walked passed it in the morning just before reaching school along Warrandyte Road, and again in the afternoon just after leaving after school on the way home. It was only about 220 yards from the school grounds. For a youngster, the sheer temptation to explore the shop's wares was just irresistible.

Imagine an entire display area devoted to confectionary, squeezed into small open trays in every conceivable space beneath a glass counter. More sweets are packed into large glass jars positioned both on top of this counter and along shelving stacked to the ceiling. Lollies were rarely packaged in those days and were sold loose and in bulk, being considerably cheaper than confectionery manufactured in wrappings.

Figure 25: Lovely lollies (© Shutterstock)

These included chocolate bullets, chocolate frogs, milk bottles, raspberries, strawberries, bananas, mint leaves, love hearts, freckles, jubes, jelly beans and jelly babies, black cats, aniseed humbugs, licorice allsorts, licorice straps, musk stix, Jersey caramels, gob-stoppers, boiled lollies in various colours, and for those seeking greater pleasure, a small white paper bag of powdered sherbet, known to youngsters as 'a bomb'. The more expensive version was the manufactured Lolly Gobble Bliss Bombs. A visual feast of colours and textures were on display for any child seeking a purchase.

Baby boomers were the first children to have pocket money after the Second World War and they knew how to be frugal with their treasures. In the 1950s, Australia's imperial currency comprised pounds, shillings and pence rather than the present decimal system. Coinage included a half-penny, a penny (equivalent to 1 cent today), a threepence (3 cents), a sixpence (equivalent value of 5 cents), a shilling (10 cents) equivalent to 12 pennies, and a florin or two shilling (20 cents). Youngsters rarely encountered currency notes as pocket money.

A penny worth of assorted sweets ('lollies') bought you quite a selection, whilst a sixpence was a relative fortune and bought you a veritable feast. The trouble was that if you actually had a sixpence in pocket money, there were suddenly many other attractive choices available to you. Icy poles, also known as 'heaven on a stick', were every child's favourite in summer, costing a mere threepence and available in a vast selection of fruit flavours and colours. They may have only been a block of flavoured ice on a stick, but what flavours! They came in raspberry, pineapple, lime, watermelon and even lemonade.

Of course sixpence could also buy you an ice cream such as the legendary Toppa's Whopper or Peter's choc wedge, or in some cases, a small bottle of fizzy soft drink such as the Victorian-manufactured Tarax or Marchants brands. Flavours available were extensive and included kola, lemon, lemonade, lime, orange, pineapple, raspberry, root beer (sarsaparilla), bitter lemon and creamy soda. Unlike today's national soft drink markets, Tarax and Marchants were only available locally in the State of Victoria at that time.

If wrapped confectionery was more to your preference, and you had slightly more pocket money, the dearer licorice Choo Choo Bar, White Knight(chocolate-coated mint-flavoured bar), Polly Waffle (waffle log chocolate bar) or Violet Crumble (chocolate-coated honeycomb) could be purchased and kept as a special treat at the movies on a Friday night or Saturday afternoon. For the serious devotee of confectionery seeking the ultimate splurge of their pocket money, sweet, sticky golden honeycomb toffee served in massive clumps in a brown paper bag would have to wait until a visit with your parents to Woolworths in Frankston.

From time to time, the tuck shop would also stock a limited range of pastries to tempt your taste buds, such as those incredible cream buns complete with a dollop of plum jam, vanilla slices, lamingtons and other exotic fare that would sell out in a single day. The next morning, another batch of assorted pastries would arrive and the exercise would simply be repeated by ravenous school children.

To my surprise, the petrol station and its shop still remain at the same location in 2017, albeit now as a Shell fuel outlet but without much discernible change from its original appearance in the 1950s. Of course, the confectionery emporium of those halcyon days would most likely be long gone.

Whilst on the important topic of pocket money, this pecuniary source had to be first earned and was rarely ever simply handed over to a child. Chores had to be completed, such as gathering bush firewood, chopping firewood, clearing house gutters of accumulated leaves and detritus, hand-feeding and watering stock (rooster, hens, a goat and any pets), cleaning the chicken coop and making beds. Errands had to be diligently fulfilled, such as collecting kerosene for lighting from the local petrol station, delivering messages to neighbours, and bringing home wild blackberries or field mushrooms. From time to time, special chores were required that were rewarded with slightly more pocket money, such as clearing vegetation on the property and cutting-back tall grass with a manual/push reel mower. Is it any wonder that as children, we truly valued our pocket money and were extremely careful about any purchases?

When one was on the long journey of primary education, you encountered many friends at various times and it was often difficult to remember them all in later life. Italian brothers Louie and Rafael Birchiolli readily come to mind for one very simple reason. They both thoroughly enjoyed playing the iconic game of marbles. In the 1950s, the marbles' craze was a childhood epidemic, much like girls' hula-hoops or the ubiquitous yoyo, requiring adept and clever skills to accomplish relatively difficult human feats of agility.

A toy marble is small, spherical and usually made from glass, agate or steel and varies in diameter between 13mm to 18mm. A tombola (also known as a Tomboller or Tom Bowler) was the largest or jumbo-sized marble at twice or thrice the size of an ordinary marble, and had a diameter of 25mm to 30mm. However, it was not always the size of the marble but the quality and condition of each piece that mattered. Players valued unchipped, striped, swirled or otherwise multi-coloured as well as unusual cat's eye marbles, and competed seriously to win them from other children.

My favourites included radiant cat's eye marbles, such as the rare purple swirls and the multi-coloured clear glass ones, dark opaques, American opaques with three colours (Agates or 'Aggies'), and the magnificent blood spotted tombolas. Many youngsters and not-so-young kids accumulated vast collections of marbles and proudly carried them around at school in bulging cloth bags for safekeeping.

Figure 26: Marvellous marbles (© Shutterstock)

One such children's game involved adding a selection of your marbles to those of the other competitor(s) on the ground inside a circle marked out at a large diameter. You would then in turn attempt to knock a competitor's marbles outside of the circle by first firmly holding a suitable marble between your first two fingers and then flicking it with your thumb as hard as possible from the perimeter. Each time you succeeded, you were awarded that competitor's marble and if skilful enough, may even dislodge other marbles from within the circle at the same time.

It would then earn you an additional attempt until failing to dislodge any more marbles, whereupon the next competitor would commence their turn. Tombolas were larger and heavier than normal marbles, and so were highly prized trophies if dislodged from the circle. Using a tombola to dislodge small marbles was a superior technique but tended to chip the glass of these smaller prizes, making them far less attractive. They were usually discouraged as 'shooting' marbles.

There were strict rules to follow that were rigidly administered when it came to fudging or cribbing. There was no 'funniking' allowable by jerking your hand forward as you 'fired your marble' during your turn. Your hand had to remain steady as the marble was flicked into the circle and not be pushed forward to gain an unfair advantage of extra momentum in striking the target marble. If you missed your target, there was no second turn. If your hand entered the circle during the shot, a severe penalty was automatic. The rules were endless but honest.

Louie, the older brother and closer to my age, was a reasonably good marble player, but Rafael the younger was a perfectionist and took some beating. I recall one particular match where Rafael used his special blue and white speckled tombola to deadly effect in dislodging many marbles. Finally his tombola was left inside the circle and I successfully dislodged it using a much smaller marble. The grand prize was mine. Not to be defeated that easily, young Rafael tried relentlessly to regain his tombola over many successive games without success, and I retained the blue and white wonder for years afterwards. The value that children placed on their hard-earned marble collections was never to be underestimated in those days.

Once the Italian brothers were driven to the school's front gate early one morning in their father's little 'bread van'. This was in the years before sliced bread had been invented. Bread packaging did not exist. All bread was baked and delivered in solid loaves, with a large loaf about twice the size of today's loaves and costing a mere threepence Their delivery van was probably more like a small truck with a flatbed tray enclosed by wire meshing within which the massive pile of loaves was securely stored. Louie and Rafael arrived sitting majestically on the very top of the pile, much like royalty riding to a bacchanalian feast of freshly-baked bread. What a couple of lovable characters. I never forgot that taste of freshly-baked bread whenever it was delivered by van.

Never saw either of them again after completing my primary school education, which was a shame for they were both likeable lads. I suppose at least one of them joined the family business just to enjoy that high quality bread.

Another of my good friends in later school years was a Greek boy named Kimon Kavadas who was also highly competitive in athletics and wrestling. I enjoyed his company immensely, particularly whenever he defeated me easily in wrestling and occasionally in athletics. His attitude to life was refreshing and realistic, accepting any loss graciously but naturally preferring to be the winner. I recall dining with his family and experiencing home-cooked Greek cuisine which was extraordinary for someone who had never tasted such variety.

His competitive spirit in everything that he attempted and his sense of justice were a great social barometer for any youngster. I lost contact with Kimon after starting secondary school in 1963, but have no doubt that he would been a success at anything that he tried, given his highly competitive nature.

Part of the pleasure of having good friends was sharing the long walk home after school along Cranbourne Road with some of them. You never knew what childhood adventures would arise along this trek, much like the fictional action hero Indiana Jones. Perhaps in certain ways, I was the alternative adventurer 'Indiana King'.

Indiana King

During the winter months, the Langwarrin district often receives substantial rainfall and as a result, a massive concrete stormwater safety drain was constructed under Cranbourne Road a short distance away from its junction with Warrandyte Road. This drain was on the route of a local stream gully which remained dry for most of the year, but following heavy rains, could rapidly become a raging torrent. The storm drain was open at both ends to permit any massive rainwater flows to safely pass under the road, as well as permit the stream's water to slowly drain across to land on the opposite side for the remainder of the year. It was also just big enough to traverse during low water flows if you stooped slightly to avoid hitting your head. In winter, it was totally inaccessible.

This drain was an excellent obstacle course for home-made matchbox marine craft constructed by my school friends. During those winter months when the torrents surged through the drain, our micro-boats would be released simultaneously on the upstream side, and an expectant group would patiently await the winner's craft to be the first to emerge across the road on the other side. I do not remember if it was by good fortune or clever nautical skills, but my matchbox boat usually at least completed the journey whereas many vessels succumbed in the drain. A simple pleasure for those days, but most enjoyable if you actually completed the course without a calamity.

As you trudged further homewards along Cranbourne Road past the storm drain, there was quite a steep rise in the road's route through a cutting with embankments on both sides. This was the perfect location for an ambush by school friends who would lie in wait for a sneak attack. This did not deter Indiana King from completing my homeward journey. Various missiles would be forthcoming from these assailants, including water bombs, moist clay/soil pats from the nearby cutting, and pine cones. A counter-attack would ensue despite the missiles raining down and the assailants would flee into the surrounding bush. Such was the enjoyment of such 'attacks', that they occurred without any form of malice or injury incurred, and were thoroughly enjoyable by all participants. If one suspected an attack was likely to occur, a short-cut through a neighbouring orchard sufficed plus provided an ample source of apples or stone-fruit in season. After all, even action heroes still had to eat. Be warned that eating out-of-season fruit can have dire circumstances and cause severe tummy-aches.

On one rare occasion, rabbits were observed in this particular orchard and chased to no avail, which was a pity as I loved rabbit stew with vegetables. Although there was an abundance of orchards throughout the district, they were rare along my homeward route. It was particularly tempting for a youngster to stray into such orchards when the fruit trees were heavily laden with apples or pears, just for a sample. In some cases, trees growing along the fenced property boundary bore so much fruit that their branches hung outside of the fence. All an adept traveller had to do was reach up and pick the fruit. It was a real shame that those orchards never produced peaches or cherries, but apples were still delicious. If these did not satisfy me on my homeward journey, there were always the plum trees grown at home.

After passing the road cutting, it was possible to enter open bushland off the road where there were no orchards, small farmlets or houses. I explored these cross country areas at will and sought out any interesting locales within the bush areas. Many unusual spots were discovered in this native bushland for further scrutiny over ensuing weekends. This delayed my homeward journey by at least another half an hour until I again returned to Cranbourne Road and approached the fringe of suburban development.

A nesting magpie occasionally took an unhealthy interest in my movement during that time and swooped without any warning. Quickly reacting like Indiana King, I avoided the relentless aerial attacks by using a dead branch to fend off the aviator until clear of its territory. Now on the home stretch, it was time to focus on reaching my house without further distraction, only to have some more friends invite you into their house nearby. Would I ever make it home in time before the 6 pm deadline for the nightly meal? Finally I would arrive home just in time for dinner, wondering where the previous three hours had gone. Such was the idyllic life of those special times in Australia.

However, there were some pitfalls in my journeys going to school in the early morning, given that this trek was over a distance of almost one mile.

More from necessity than choice, I walked to school along Cranbourne Road and then the short distance along Warrandyte Road every weekday morning, leaving at least an hour or more before the start of school. I called it 'the long lonely trek'. We never had a reliable vehicle nor functional bicycles as a family, and so commonly used Shank's pony (walked) as there was no scheduled bus service that early in the morning heading towards Cranbourne. Although Cranbourne Road was sealed with bitumen, it did not have any established footpaths, so I simply walked along the gravel edging beside the road in the direction of oncoming traffic to be safest.

In my early years of primary school until 1959, my older sister joined me on this lengthy trek which made for great companionship. On one very rare occasion, we were actually driven to school in my father's old 1920s open-topped Chrysler sedan, complete with running boards along each side. The ageing vehicle no longer possessed a canvas top and was now truly a convertible. It had to be started by manually turning a metal starter rod inserted through a grille opening at the front of the vehicle that cranked the engine into action. Once operational, it would take some stopping. With my sister standing on one running board and myself on the other, tightly gripping the sides, we progressed slowly along the road at a top speed sometimes up to 25 miles per hour, decreasing to a snail's pace of walking speed when encountering any uphill sections. As I recollect, we passed no other cars that morning on the short journey as it was rare to encounter many vehicles around Langwarrin in the early to mid-1950s.

As my father aged and his health deteriorated, the old Chrysler was only driven infrequently, perhaps to collect the family on a Friday night from the Frankston Picture Theatre or to take delivery of an order of lumber in town. By the early 1960s, it became a permanent fixture on the property, with tyres completely deflated and covered in accumulated dust and leaves. The final end came when it was unceremoniously removed for scrap metal by a dealer to whom we paid the sum of £5. Being somewhat frugal, my father managed to remove a few essential automotive parts from the vehicle before the day as keepsakes. In today's terms, such a vintage automobile would command a magnificent fee for only minimal restoration cost. Such were those times that one rarely thought about future events and the true value of historical assets.

Strange as it may appear, walking to school in the fresh brisk mornings was quite enjoyable and decidedly healthy. It was only the odd encounters that made it somewhat disconcerting. Inclement weather was always a potential problem, particularly on blustery, wind-swept days when the strong gusts would almost knock you over at times. Heavy soaking rains and cold temperatures would be another drawback, despite how many raincoats that I wore. The odd thunderstorm with lightning strikes never helped much either. Nonetheless, it taught me independence, resolve and the motivation to continue on regardless; all the essential survival skills that Indiana King required. The only problem was trying to dry out in front of the heaters at school in time before classes commenced.

Magpie nesting season was another arduous hazard sometimes encountered on the journey, which meant carrying a very large stick to fend off any aerial attack. This would occur within about a 100 yard radius of a magpie nest and the incessant swooping would be relentless and ruthless. Those birds certainly had mastered the art of silent ambush to perfection. One unfortunate incident occurred when I encountered Michael, a local boy much younger than myself, being attacked with the magpie still perched on his head. With blood trickling down his face, the young boy must have been in total shock as he did nothing to prevent the ongoing assault by the bird. One swipe from my wooden stick frightened the magpie sufficiently for it to relent and retreat to nearby trees. The boy recovered quickly after suitable medical treatment at the school and we eventually became close friends after that traumatic day.

Wildlife distractions along the route were plentiful in those days and very rewarding as well. Along the short stretch of Warrandyte Road between Cranbourne Road and school, there were several mature age eucalyptus trees growing along one side of the road. In the branches of these trees at various times, there were flocks of kookaburras creating considering havoc and riotous noise from their distinctive bird calls, and occasionally koalas hidden amongst the foliage. Over the years, koalas were prolific in those trees and undisturbed by the passing traffic or progressive urban encroachment.

Only once over so many years of walking the journey did I encounter 'stranger danger', when a passing motorist stopped and offered me sweets. I simply remained on the opposite side of the road to his vehicle and walked on. Realising that I was not interested, he promptly drove away. Living in the bush always gave me a sense of preparedness to anticipate just about anything. This included an acute sense of vehicle awareness when walking along road verges throughout the district which I did frequently as there were rarely any designated footpaths. Fortunately at primary school, this 'road sense' was reinforced constantly by the following tried and true safety method; 'If crossing a road, stop, look left first, then look right and finally look left again for any traffic before crossing.' It worked successfully every single time for me. Another basic but effective survival skill learned in those early formative years.

Fast forward to the mid-1990s when I returned to my local district of Langwarrin to visit the family home, and decided to retrace this journey on foot along Cranbourne Road, past the local Tuck Shop and up the rise of Warrandyte Road to my old primary school. It was a daunting but sentimental trek with the urban sprawl everywhere. Gone were the original bushland locations so clear in my memory, replaced by row upon row of houses, concrete footpaths and incessant vehicular traffic. The Cranbourne-Frankston Road was now a major thoroughfare and impossible to traverse safely by foot. At least the school would be intact, I thought.

To my considerable disappointment, I discovered a vacant block of land where the school had originally been located. Gone was every building and sign of human occupation, with only the front cyclone mesh fence still evident to stop trespassers. Indiana King was not impressed. A new and larger primary school had been constructed further along Warrandyte Road on the opposite side of the road. I did not bother to visit it, but rather spent a wonderful hour reminiscing on the vacant block where the classrooms, the shelter shed and the netball court would have been, as well as that grassed sports ground. So many wonderful memories are all that remain today of this delightful school and that long lonely trek every weekday morning.

Fetes, Halls and Parties

The 1950s were a remarkable time for people in a community to socialise in person without the superfluous distractions so prevalent in the modern era, such as television, computers, mobile phones and the Internet. Communication was normally face-to-face and an enjoyable experience shared by one and all. People became involved in special community events, willingly contributed their time to assist where so required, and expected nothing whatsoever in return. School, church or hospital fetes convened to raise funds for essential services or charitable causes were amongst the most popular.

Fetes (fairs) were typically held outdoors and provided entertainment as well as a diverse range of saleable local produce, goods and refreshments to satisfy even the most disinterested visitor. The primary school fetes were legendary, with a prolific choice of quality homemade sweets, including toffee apples, toffee topped with shredded coconut or rainbow sprinkles ('hundreds and thousands') in cupcake patty pans, likewise baked chocolate Coco-Pops in paper patty pans and coconut ice slices.

Cake stalls were one of my favourites with sponge cakes topped with freshly whipped cream, layers of fresh lamingtons and every possible combination of fruit cake. There was also an interesting range of currant buns, sticky date pudding slices and vanilla slices. For liquid refreshment, homemade cordials with fresh fruit included were always most popular. I take this opportunity to also mention the iconic Australian meat pie and its popular overseas cousin, the Cornish pastie. Homemade vegetable pasties sold at district fetes were irresistible to me, lovingly baked with fresh local produce in a light crusty pastry that was a delight to consume. Even the trusty 'Four 'N Twenty' classic meat pies were delectable and always served with tomato sauce. Perhaps it was the quality of the butcher's meat in those days or even the extra-light pastry, but it was always difficult for me to resist. Just listen to the 18th century ancient nursery rhyme *Sing a song of six-pence* to savour the meat pie experience:

> Sing a song of sixpence,
> A pocket full of rye;
> Four and twenty blackbirds
> baked in a pie.
>
> When the pie was opened
> The birds began to sing;
> Wasn't that a dainty dish
> To set before the King![1]

In the modern era, the diversity of such meat pies is astounding and caters to gourmet tastes. Notwithstanding, the thought of all those blackbirds in a pie did not deter me for one instant from making the important childhood decision to purchase a meat pie.

I usually entered every competition available at these fetes by purchasing at least one ticket and sometimes several at ridiculously low prices; five tickets for a shilling, for example. The donated prizes were often very generous and worthy of winning. Even guessing the number of jelly beans in a large glass jar or perhaps the weight of an enormous pumpkin to the nearest ounce was quite a challenge. The best competition of all was clearly the Lucky Dip, where for a nominal fee I was likely to win anything from a useless booby prize to an expensive fountain pen. Imagine a substantial empty wine cask or oversized wooden beer barrel filled to the brim with sawdust. Inside this container were innumerable small gifts, trinkets and novelties tightly wrapped in multiple layers of brown paper to disguise their true value.

After paying a modest fee, I dug deep into the barrel and foraged around for any of these packages until securing one that definitely felt interesting in shape. I retrieved it and upon unwrapping the surprise, discovered some useful pencil sharpeners, lead pencils and a rubber. The person next to me retrieved a bag of confectionery, and the next fellow found one unused balloon, much to his annoyance. Occasionally, an expensive treasure would emerge for a lucky person, such as an alarm clock or even a wrist watch.

In some respects, fetes were not unlike jumble sales or 'white elephant stalls' where all sorts of knick-knacks and second-hand items were purchased, such as comics, adventure books, fairy tale books, toys, gardening tools, or original knitwear made by parents such as beanies, scarfs and cardigans. It was incredible what treasures and bargains could be found on those stalls. There were bottled home-made flavoured chutney, pickled onions, pickles, unusual fruits and vegetables, jams of every possible type (marmalade, fig, plum, cumquat, strawberry and of course blackberry), local honey, and various sizes of free range eggs (bantam up to jumbo). Some farmers also seized the opportunity to sell smaller farm stock such as kittens, puppies, domesticated chicks, ducklings and even eels.

Gymkhanas were occasionally held in the district as many locals still owned horses, and these community gatherings were often a combination of ad hoc equestrian events, carnival rides and novelty races for the crowd. It was all about having fun, similar to country agricultural shows still convened today. I recall being awarded an expensive travel clock at one such gymkhana by winning the 100 yard sprint against all comers, running barefoot on dry parched grass that was extremely harsh on the soles of my feet.

Sack races were downright hilarious, with two people sharing each heavy, thick burlap (jute) bag and trying to foolishly synchronise their co-ordinated jumping techniques whilst still tightly gripping the bag, without falling over or colliding with other contestants. When one person occupied a jute sack, the correct technique was to position your toes in each corner of the sack and stagger along without tripping over. When two people squeezed into a sack, it became a concerted mutual effort of hopping, often with dire consequences. If any team actually made it the finishing line, they truly deserved the prize. Sometimes a visiting cowboy would be asked to provide some fancy exhibitions for the crowd by whip-cracking and flicking a cigarette out of someone's mouth without causing any harm. Of course, the poor volunteer had to stand side-ways to the whip-cracker, otherwise it was highly likely that one's nose might be removed by the tip of the whip instead of the cigarette.

The original Langwarrin District Hall (now integrated with the Men's Shed at Langwarrin Hub) located just off Cranbourne Road on a small offset lane at the end of Warrandyte Road, was the venue in the district for most community indoor social gatherings. This iconic hall featured well-attended old time ballroom dances most Saturday evenings, fancy dress and debutante balls, sporting presentation nights, primary school concerts and even flower shows on some weekends. On 7th August 1964, my only sister was one of ten local girls and their partners at the Langwarrin Football Club Debutante Ball to be presented to Dame Elizabeth Murdoch.[2] These were memorable special occasions as the district's young women, dressed in fabulous ball gowns, stepped out for the first time in public as young adults.

Figure 27: Langwarrin public hall on Cranbourne Road

(Ric Norman, Mornington Peninsula Family Historical Society)

The ballroom dances required everyone bring a mandatory plate of hearty refreshments such as sandwiches, cakes, scones, buttered pikelets or savoury biscuits with many different fillings, and expected most people to dress for the occasion. A three or four piece professional brass band, such as the *Silver Star Band*, played throughout the evening with all the patrons comfortably seated around the walls of the hall. Once the music was underway, the dance floor soon became crowded, and for communal dances like the Progressive Waltz for example, a massive circle of dancers would rotate through innumerable partners, exchanging them in turn for the next in the circle. Meanwhile youngsters and the not-so-young uninterested in dancing had absconded to the carpark, where the children could play hide and seek out in the darkness until supper was served around 9 pm. Hot tea was served in proper cups and saucers, accompanied by that incredible choice of food. It was definitely a unique time to greet old friends and acquaintances as well as make many new friends. I even learned to formally dance from the quickstep to the waltz, despite being so young.

The music was variable and upbeat most of the time, and certainly kept people on the dance floor. Many of the delightful young ladies barely had the opportunity to be seated before being asked for the next dance by yet another partner. These splendid dances may have appeared somewhat 'old fashioned' to outside visitors, but such old-world charm and customs are now all but extinct in the modern era. The semi-formal dances provided a great opportunity to 'dress-up' just for the evening, mingle with your local community and thoroughly enjoy yourself on a Saturday night without any concerns about personal safety or unprovoked violence. A rare bygone time indeed.

In late 1971, as a young man barely 21 years of age, I took my new girlfriend to the ballroom dance at the hall to acquaint her with this unique experience after an absence of several years. I found it almost unchanged. Strange that the hall seemed so spacious and its carpark so enormous to a youngster in the 1950s, and yet as an adult, it now seemed so remarkably small. Never mind; the fabulous spread of home-baked refreshments for supper was still the same, and that was more important to me.

Gala events convened in the Langwarrin Hall also included fancy dress functions, where a certain element of mystery was involved in trying to identify various individuals despite the intricate camouflage of their costumes and masks. The level of artisan skill, imagination and flair that went into crafting such homemade costumes in those days was truly amazing. There were no fancy dress hire companies – only devoted mothers who spent endless hours creating artistic works of extravagance just for a primary school special night. My favourite costume was as Sir Lancelot from King Arthur's Court, resplendent in regal attire, shiny cardboard shield and wooden sword. My lustrous golden cardboard helmet was suitably flexible enough to hide my face, leaving all to guess who was behind the mask.

Eventually after much guesswork, all was revealed when the night's best costume prizes would be awarded, and the various children would unmask, if their fancy costumes lasted that long. Outside, in the darkness of the carpark, many a minor scuffle or fracas would ensue between children, anxious to prevent potential rivals from gaining any ascendancy. Bedraggled and dishevelled children with only partial costumes remaining sheepishly returned to the hall and ultimately realised that there could never be a prize for them in that advanced state of deterioration. I mean, what was a robot once its antennae was broken and its articulated arms disconnected from the torso?

Prizes were always more than simply awards, but rather an accolade or recognition of one's mother and her extreme diligence in preparing such an artistic creation. I am confident that such nights were special because everyone came with the same community spirit of participation for thorough enjoyment. Sadly, such days are long past but hopefully, the spirit of endeavour and camaraderie endures.

A rather unique community custom traditionally held in Langwarrin each year either in early or late summer when days were the longest and not excessively hot was the progressive dinner. This custom was held commencing in the late afternoon and involved a mixed group of like-minded local people of all ages who visited several houses across the district on foot. At each venue, a different home-made course of food would be served to those managing the long walk. First course was typically a flavoursome vegetable soup complete with fresh crusty bread. At the next house, a suitable entrée of some rich fish/beef/chicken serving was dished up. At successive houses thereafter, a main course — perhaps a roast or stew, a delicious dessert, and finally at the last house, cheese and dry biscuits, sweet biscuits, scones and fresh cream as well as tea and coffee. The leisurely intervening walks gave the diners adequate time for a digestive break between courses and for conversing with each other.

Distances between houses varied widely and I suppose on average were probably less than half a mile, but on a balmy summer evening strolling along lonely country roads with no traffic at all, what did it really matter? I made many new acquaintances in the group walking between each house anticipating what the next culinary course provided might be, passed familiar faces along the way and most all, had a great time. By the time it was over around 9 pm, it was actually almost dark, but who cared after such great company and even better, freshly prepared food?

What made youngsters' birthday parties extra special in the 50s was not all the fancy and expensive treats so prolific today, such as petting 'zoos' of cuddly or exotic animals like llamas, hired inflatable bouncy castles, or mega-dollar birthday cakes. It was so much more important than price, or experiencing the bizarre. It was simplicity, such as crinkly translucent gift wrapping paper in vivid, almost electric colours like rose, violet or chocolate. The gift wrapping was almost an art form in itself. It was receiving an unexpected present from someone that you never really liked but invited anyway. It was about everyone having a great time without expecting anything else.

It was about a special day, not just for the recipient but for all the young guests, and not having to impress anyone, particularly your parents. Perhaps most significantly, it was a day when you could be yourself without those irritating overriding conditions of adulthood – discipline and manners.

One year I shared the celebration of my seventh birthday (30th October) with that of my best school friend Alan Cater on his birthday of 31st October at his house. His parents spared no effort in providing every possible type of birthday food and drink. His birthday gift to me was equally thoughtful, whereas my gift to him was home-made, yet he later confided it was extraordinary. Sometimes, it is simply not possible to buy everything. Alan left Langwarrin primary school well before 1962 so I presumed that he also left the district, which was disappointing for me to lose such a great friend. We shared many common interests and were extremely close for a few short years. Such close friends were quite rare in my childhood.

One very special gift that I once received for my birthday was a toy cap-pistol resembling an old western Colt 45 handgun, and an ample supply of rolls of caps. At least when I played Cowboys and Indians, I did not run out of ammunition. Rarely did anyone want to play the part of the native North American Indian, although one child came to my birthday dressed for the role, complete with a spectacular headdress and a bow and arrow set. Fortunately the arrow heads were not pointed and dangerous, but had small suction cups attached so that the arrow stuck to me when it landed, just for that extra embarrassment of being 'killed by the Indians'. When I was a guest at another child's birthday party and it was time to nominate sides for Cowboys and Indians, I always ensured that I came prepared with own toy gun, holster and hat.

I never left a children's birthday party in the 50s without the mandatory white paper bag overflowing with various sweets, and of course, a piece of the birthday cake carefully wrapped in paper serviettes by the host's parents. If the birthday child liked you, a complimentary balloon went home with you as well. Birthday cakes in those days were either resplendent in decorative frosty icing or simply a large homemade cream sponge cake amply embossed with the name and age of the birthday boy or girl in icing sugar and obligatory candles. It did not really matter to me as it was always delicious cake with enough for everyone.

The food was always delicious. I started with cocktail frankfurts drowning in tomato sauce followed by fairy bread (thin slices of buttered fresh bread cut into halves and sprinkled with multi-coloured 'hundreds and thousands'), butterfly cakes and the obligatory chocolate crackles made with

Rice Bubbles, cocoa, coconut and copha.[3] These were complemented by fudge slices, toffee in cupcake patties sprinkled with more 'hundreds and thousands', various other smaller cakes (vanilla slices, cupcakes, cream puffs with plum jam, and sometimes even chocolate eclairs). It was every child's gastronomic dream, finished off with flavoured ice-cream and fruit jelly towards the end of the party. Flavoured cordial or lemonade were always in copious supply.

Each party game involved a prize. At Alan's birthday in particular, some of the prizes were quite expensive. We played pass the parcel, blind man's bluff, pin the tail on the donkey, musical chairs and the ever popular hide and seek where we had to reach home base without being tagged. These were special days and only came along infrequently, but most children tended to have at least one such birthday party between the ages of 7 and 12 as I recollect. Most children also usually went home with a prize or two. Looking back, it is almost as if the party games were somehow fixed by the adults to ensure that no-one left disappointed and not simply based upon chance.

Saturday Sport and Quiet Sundays

Every young boy in those times wanted to play Australian ('Aussie') Rules football in winter, and cricket in the warmer summer period, which neatly dovetailed with the end of the football season anyway. As a result, it was obligatory to own a pair of football boots and a hand-crafted willow cricket bat, usually autographed by a famous Australian cricketer of the times, such as Bobby Simpson. The boots contained wooden stops/studs carefully nailed in a tight sequence to the underside of each boot for ground-gripping purposes, rather than the moulded plastic studs integral to the boots of the modern era. If any of the wooden stops split and exposed a nail, the boots suddenly took on a new purpose altogether.

Many a time I returned from a vigorous match with various scratch marks across my back from such boots as an opposition player tried to mark the football by jumping over me. As I traditionally played in the defensive role of the full back as a youngster (similar to a goal keeper in soccer), my injuries were so consistent that my mother often thought that I had been brawling rather than playing football.

I played Aussie Rules throughout my primary school years and eventually at the local Langwarrin Football Ground at Lloyd Park Reserve, across Cranbourne Road and up the hill at the opposite end of Warrandyte Road to the school. This ground was located on the edge of an extensive operational sand quarry, and the oval was more sand than grass, with the occasional rabbit burrow to boot. Training involved relentlessly running up and down and up and down nearby 30 metre high, near-vertical sand dunes, regardless of the weather or the time of night. Cold showers in the middle of winter on freezing blustery evenings were an extra treat if the hot water system had not been ignited in time for the training session.

Our change rooms were an old green shed aptly named 'the Tin Shed' that had been relocated to Lloyd Park in two sections and reassembled. This shed had quite a past, originally having been in use by troops during World War 2 and subsequently serving as a hostel for migrants.[1] In those times at Lloyd Park, there were usually only one or two floodlights operating, so when the football was kicked beyond the floodlit area, it meant searching for the ball in total darkness. There was little to be gained from trying to retrieve the ball quickly due to the possibility of tripping over a rabbit burrow and potentially twisting an ankle.

Our junior football team had the unenviable reputation of rarely winning a game season after painful season, despite having a well-balanced team of reasonably fit and talented players. I was selected to play as the team's full back, possibly because most our matches were played predominantly defending at that end of the ground. In one extreme example whilst playing away against the Red Hill football team who kicked 32 goals against us that day, the only reason that we scored at all was that one of our players was unceremoniously carried across the goal line by the opposition. This ensured that a single point was allocated as our only score, and the Red Hill team's winning percentage was thus able to be calculated.

Of course, the downside of being the team's full back was that you were required to kick the football back into play from your goal square every time the opposition had scored a point. It was your responsibility to ensure the kick went to one of our team and well clear of the opposition's scoring area. Sometimes this did not go to plan, and the opposition simply returned the favour by kicking a goal over my head. To overcome this possibility, I developed a strategy to always use the spiral torpedo punt kick, known as 'a torp'.

This meant holding the football at a slight offset angle to your proposed kicking direction, which resulted in the ball spiralling through the air and usually travelling considerably more distance than achieved by other kicks. On a particularly gusty day with a strong, howling wind prevailing up the football ground towards our scoring end, I opted to wait those few precious seconds for the next mighty gust of wind to assist my torpedo kick. With a gust of wind so strong that it almost bowled me over, I kicked the football ferociously and it sailed skywards spiralling to perfection.

Then the wind gust lifted the ball, and it flew on and on and on. The football eventually landed well past the centre of the ground but continued onwards, bouncing violently and still propelled by the wind. It bounced past at least two opposition players and was not far from our goals before it was finally stopped in its tracks. I could have been the only full back to have famously scored from a kick-out at the opposite end of the ground on that windy day. Of course, when a full back had to 'kick into the wind', it became pointless to use the torp, as the wind simply acted as a barrier. I had to kick the ball as low to the ground as possible to minimise the resistance of the wind.

A particular kick that a full back player never used was the infamous drop 'stab' kick due to its unreliability. This precise kick required considerable skill by the kicker to hold the football vertically and to drop the ball to the ground whilst 'stabbing' it with your toe in one synchronised motion. If successful, the ball would strike the ground just as you struck the football, projecting it ferociously at low height precisely to your intended target. If unsuccessful, your toe either kicked the ground instead or the football simply rolled along the ground (eloquently known as 'grubbing the football'). In later years, the drop punt unfortunately replaced this highly skilled technique due to its lower risk of failure of execution.

I am unsure if the football boots of the 50s and 60s contributed to my kicking prowess, but given they were high-backed and made of tough, resilient real leather, they must have been better than today's low-cut synthetic 'boots' that do not cover the ankle and are akin to ergonomic cleats or elite sports 'shoes'. Given that the boots of my childhood were laced high up the foot well above the ankle for protection, it allowed the kicker to maximise contact with the football. The result was the perfect recipe for delivering a diversity of penetrating drop kicks, precision stab passes and towering torpedo punts. I must also mention that because of the wooden studs and the thick leather composition of the boot, they were also quite heavy to wear, and even more so when wet. The upside of this dilemma was when kicking the ball, the boot certainly produced a very powerful kick.

Although I was usually selected to play as defender, on occasion I was used in the forward zone and sometimes scored goals. The elation for a youngster in scoring for your team was invigorating. I only ever played in finals football in one season and it was electric. However, my more enjoyable sporting times were definitely whilst still at primary school.

The most famous footballer to attend the primary school in my time was Leigh Mathews, who was in the grade below me, and who always seemed to play as a rover (midfielder in the modern era) in our school football matches. I understand that he left the district in 1962. Leigh eventually went on the play as a rover at the highest level of Aussie Rules with the Hawthorn Football Club during 1969-1985, and ultimately became a celebrated coach by winning four national football premierships at two different clubs. The national competition since named him as the Player of the Century and he became an inductee of their Hall of Fame.[2] It was memorable to play alongside this very talented person, particularly during school Lightning premierships/carnivals.

These one day tournaments involved several schools participating in brief football matches lasting perhaps 30 to 40 minutes, causing a mad scramble to score anything in the severely restricted time allocated. Groups of schools played each other in turn, but only the winners continued to advance to the finals. Local school football matches were not as frenetic but Leigh's presence in the team always provided us with some positive hope of winning. His tenacity and skills were evident in every single game, and in many cases, greatly assisted our team endeavours.

I once attended a local football game merely as an interested spectator when I was about 14 or 15 years of age, and learned that one of the team's selected players had not arrived. The coach enquired if I could join the game and I accepted without a second thought. Despite wearing a pair of borrowed football boots one size too small for me, I kicked six goals for my adopted team and was voted best afield for the match. Unfortunately, when removing my boots after the game, I realised that much of the skin on both feet had been severely chafed by the undersized boots. As I hobbled home, I wondered if my mother would conclude that I had been brawling again.

All too soon, the summer cricket season commenced and it was time to store away the football boots and start wearing the obligatory white apparel (shirt, floppy hat, trousers and shoes) essential to play junior cricket. The willow bat was seasoned with light oil and it was off to many far flung and relatively obscure locations, such as Upper Beaconsfield, Koo Wee Rup or Tooradin. Of course, one still needed to train each week, and on one particular afternoon I walked into the bush adjacent to the local oval to retrieve a cricket ball.

Looking for a small cricket ball in dense scrub was a difficult task, even without encountering a large, highly venomous and rampant tiger snake. This was to be my second encounter with a tiger snake, having carefully avoided another one near my home years before. These snakes are particularly agile and able to lunge quite a distance at their victims without warning. Slowly, ever so painstakingly slowly, I cautiously retreated from the snake which slithered away without attacking. I left that ball in the bush permanently.

Playing junior cricket in the early 60s meant anything could happen, and on one visit to a neighbouring district, our team was taught quite a lesson in cricket. In our first innings, our team only managed to score fewer than twenty runs, due to an exceptionally fast bowler on the other team. Thinking that it was simply bad luck, we were soon to discover this was not the case, only managing a mere 10 runs in our second innings. Their young bowler was so fast that I never saw the ball coming, let alone it removing the stumps behind me. I wondered how long before the football season recommenced.

We were most fortunate to have an excellent wicket keeper in our team through those years, who was also adept at making runs as well. His severe disability from a birth defect (possibly from spina bifida) meant his legs did not develop normally and thus restricted his ability to walk without considerable effort, or to run at all. To compensate, he developed his upper body strength and agility to the extent that no ball would bypass him. Many an opposition player was caught outside the batting crease and stumped by our keeper, who became expert at crouching directly behind the cricket stumps.

When it was time for our team to bat and the keeper took his turn, he simply had a substitute team member to run between wickets as 'his runner'. Many games were won thanks to his perseverance and tenacity to overcome his physical disability, which in some ways highlighted the value of self-motivation to the remainder of the team.

The routine of playing under-16s junior cricket across two consecutive Saturday mornings was augmented by the dedication and encouragement of our local district sports stalwart Richard 'Dick' Cavill. '...Dick would pick up all the boys at the corner of Warrandyte and Cranbourne Roads at 8 am and take them to their game in his 8-seater Combi van. They would be back for lunch...'[3]

Not only was Dick our coach and mentor, but he was the Club President and eventually made a Life Member of the local cricket club (and football club), as was his wife who acted as tea lady, fundraiser and of course, team scorer. I recall that Dick was a very talented spin bowler at training and spent considerable time developing the skills of cricket amongst all my teammates. Because of his dedication, training sessions were something special and not to be missed. Such was the community spirit of playing cricket in a semi-rural environment where you were provided with every opportunity to develop.

Why did so many Australians choose to attend Sunday church services every week or at least several times a year in the 50s, including our family? The reasons are probably quite simple and had much to do with respectability in the community. As a rule, most children of that era were raised to be clean, neat and well-dressed out of respect for their parents and to indicate the same to the community. It was obligatory for many children to attend church in order to gain some religious training apart from that already provided in their primary school education. Most Australians went to church because 'it was the right thing to do'.[4]

Langwarrin had two churches (Methodist and St Thomas' Church of England) dating from around the time of the First World War, although their locations in the district sometimes changed according to circumstances, including bushfires, funding arrangements, available land at various times and other matters. Notwithstanding, Sundays were always a non-work day and attendance at church customary for many local residents of the parish. I recall attending many crowded services wearing my best 'going-out' clothing and quietly listening to sermons, in awe of proceedings. Afterwards, upcoming church events such as charity fetes or local community news were discussed with the congregation, much like an extended family. Times were far less complicated than nowadays, and many parishioners not only shared spiritual guidance but an interest in the community's development.

For a youngster, the rest of Sunday was free time spent exploring across the countryside, visiting a neighbour's children, or possibly just spending the day at home. It is probably best to acknowledge here that children's clothing in those days was designed to be practical rather than fashionable, predominantly due to cost.

> In the post-war period [after the Second World War], with the lifting of clothing rationing… clothes became more extravagant. This had little effect on the style of children's clothing. The average child's wardrobe remained relatively modest, consisting largely of homemade or hand-me-downs. Each child had three sets of clothes – play clothes, school clothes and the 'going-out' outfit. Warm sensible clothing was the keynote.[5]

My mother always taught us to be frugal with everything that we owned, including our clothing, shoes and anything else of value. If it was becoming frayed, shabby or falling to pieces, it would be repaired, patched, sewn, mended or even reused in some other way, and rarely discarded. She also made much of our clothing from rolls of material fabric using her Singer sewing machine. The bulk fabric was prudently purchased during store sale periods and judiciously stored away for later times. Fashion never came into the equation and second-hand items were always preferred over new purchases. The rule applied to most of our possessions and was a lesson learnt for life. Unlike the rampant consumerism of the modern era where many people only want new items, our lives revolved around making the most of what necessities you were given as children – it was a sensible approach to make everything last longer.

I only ever had two types of clothing; my 'going-out' outfit, and everything else. During the winter months, the former outfit included a small British-style buttoned coat with a velvet collar that I avoided wearing wherever possible. It gave me a rather fancy and regal appearance, much like *Little Lord Fauntleroy* portrayed in the famous 19th century children's novel of the same name, until I slipped over and fell in the mud of course. Needless to say, that coat did not last long given the arduous circumstances experienced in winter. Nightwear also demands some recognition at this time, given the contemporary popularity of pyjamas. Unfortunately, my nightwear included an oversized single-piece, neck-high, flannel/woollen nightgown which was great in winter but claustrophobic if worn in summer.

In today's modern era, 50s apparel is often considered to be desirable retro or vintage clothing. As a child, I always embraced wearing tee-shirts which still remain very fashionable after all these years. The variety of colours and designs was phenomenal for such a simple and affordable garment, and yet as children, we always seemed to have several in our wardrobe. Other clothing certainly not as remarkable but definitely making a statement were jodhpurs and duffle coats, with the latter only becoming popular from the early 60s. Our family never owned a horse and probably had never ridden one, yet jodhpurs were definitely a fashion statement in Australia for horse riding.

These vintage pants were baggy between the waist and the knee, and thereafter tight-fitting to the ankle, ending in a snug cuff. If someone owned a horse, they were seen in this apparel without question. If not, jodhpurs were still worn in winter for their warmth and baggy comfort factor. Duffle coats on the other hand were popular in winter with just about everyone in their teenage years and younger. By the early 1960s, my older brother, my sister and I each owned a duffle coat. The following description probably identifies why they became so popular:

> … made of dense woollen cloth, and distinctive features including a capacious hood that can be worn over a uniform cap, three or four wood or horn toggles with leather loops for ease of fastening when wearing gloves, a buttonable strap neck and two

large outside patch pockets.[6]

Children's shoes were an entirely different proposition. With limited funds to replace worn shoes, our family were regular visitors to the shoe repair shop in Frankston which was particularly adept at replacing heels, patching over the inevitable holes in the soles of your shoes and providing any other upkeep requiring those special bootmaker glues or microscopic tacks. New shoes were rare indeed, and only purchased after every other possible alternative had been investigated. After all, even a reasonable pair of second-hand shoes still went a long way. Shoes were made of leather and required daily cleaning, polishing and buffing by hand to maintain them. When the big day finally arrived to purchase a new pair of shoes, usually for walking between home and primary school, it was off to nearby Frankston again.

Fortunately, the Bata Shoe Company had established a production facility on the Mornington Peninsula by December 1961 and manufactured a generous supply of quality footwear locally, spoiling us for choice and price. I am unsure if the smell of new shoes overwhelmed my senses or it was simply the delight of wearing them, but trying to determine the correct fit was always a dilemma. Once I had selected the right colour (usually black) and size, it was a matter of walking up and down inside the shop for comfort. This brief 'road test' was pivotal to the final decision to purchase, and often it was difficult given the plush soft carpeting underfoot masking the comfort factor.

Why could I not walk along a gravel road first for about a mile just to be sure they were still comfortable? If they appeared too tight initially, the salesman assured me they would just need to be worn for a while to suit. Hours later and with blisters forming on both my heels, I usually regretted taking his advice as I hobbled along. Selecting a pair of Dunlop canvas sandshoes for sporting events was a far easier task, but even they required regular scrubbing and occasional coating with Kiwi/Nugget shoe whitener to maintain that important new look.

Going to Town

The distance between our house and the nearest large town of Frankston by road was substantial, and due to the unreliability of our family car, it typically meant there were only two suitable choices of transport. A private bus company operated a limited weekday daily service, usually comprising an early morning, lunchtime and late afternoon return trip to Frankston. However, travelling by 'Shank's pony' using your own legs to walk the distance was often the only choice remaining, particularly on weekends. If one was fortunate, a passing motorist might stop and offer a lift into town, but traffic was quite infrequent along that road back then.

The town of Frankston was markedly different to anywhere else that I had experienced as a youngster. It had an immense diversity and number of retail shops, larger variety stores, pharmacies, hairdressing salons, banks, schools, public buildings, several churches, some hotels, factories and petrol stations, parks, a picture theatre, a beach with a pier, and an operating railway station at the end of the train line from Melbourne, and yet was directly adjoining rural community areas. The following description adds further insight:

> Frankston's history is unusual. The township, established in 1854, has never quite been able to distinguish whether it is a country town servicing its hinterland, a pleasure resort, a dormitory suburb for Melbourne, the gateway to the Mornington Peninsula, or a self-contained city with its own employment and retail centres.[1]

Family shopping excursions into Frankston were strictly on an occasional basis for replenishment of food supplies and seeking essential timber and hardware goods not readily available in semi-rural areas. Eventually, once overloaded with our precious items, we would be treated to a return bus ride home and delivered right to our driveway. This was a luxury rarely provided in our family, as walking was always the preferred mode of travel.

My distinct recollection of Frankston in the late 50s was that of a bustling seaside town with endless streets of shops, department stores and cafes, as well as entertainment areas such as a cinema, ten pin bowling alley and so much more. On weekdays, it was a hub of activity for the local district whereas on weekends after noon on Saturday when most shops closed, it became mostly deserted. Groups of youths frequented the streets at those times in search of entertainment, perhaps simply waiting for the nightlife to commence in the town.

My favourite family outing as a youngster was always the Friday night pictures at Frankston's original Plaza Picture Theatre first constructed in Playne Street in the earlier part of the 20th century.

Figure 28: Opening of Frankston Picture Theatre, circa 1920 -1930s in Playne Street (Frankston City Libraries, Frankston Town Centre Album LHV7, p.9)

It was far more than simply 'going to the pictures', and involved several crucial stages of entertainment. In those days when the family's old car was still operational, my father actually drove the family into town late in the afternoon and then returned home. Other times, it meant using the local bus service. Our little group then wended our way to the local 'fish & chips' takeaway shop near the foreshore and ordered a huge serving of fresh flake (young shark) coated in flour batter, deep fried potato chips, potato cakes (patties) and pickled onions, generously flavoured with sea salt and drenched in vinegar.

With the simmering meal suitably insulated by several layers of butcher's white paper, we strolled to the nearby pier or sometimes onto the beach for our ravenous feed. Like a flock of swarming seagulls, numerous small hands appeared once the meal was unwrapped, and fragments of torn fish, long thick chips and small slippery onions disappeared from sight in the ensuing feeding frenzy. Next, it was time for a refreshing dessert.

After another short stroll from the foreshore into town, we arrived at our favourite local Greek café near the cinema. Cafes in the late 1950s did not really provide outdoor seating, but offered a series of compact bench seats tightly squeezed along the interior walls. We selected this café as it made the best flavoured milkshakes in town with generous servings of ice-cream and fruit topping, despite the incredibly cramped seating arrangement. Being spoiled for choice, we could have also ordered a sweet ice cream dessert known as a sundae. These lavish desserts comprised generous scoops of ice cream covered in thick flavoured syrup, such as caramel or strawberry, and topped with whipped cream, sprinklings of finely ground nuts, maraschino cherries or other suitable fruits. The décor of this café was most impressive and reflected the proud cultural heritage of the owners.

Perhaps we should have ordered café hamburgers in 1955 instead:

> … has to be made in a small shop, probably a milk-bar, run by an Italian or Greek family, with the mum and children often sitting on stools out of the way. The dad has to be sweaty, standing over a hotplate, taking orders over his shoulder, while a son or daughter chops the beetroot, tomato and onion, and wraps up the

> end product. The meat has to be proper minced meat, with real-blood dripping off the wooden cutting-board. The beetroot is essential, and it has to be so fresh that its juice will dribble down onto your shirt at the first bite. No hamburger is complete without burnt onion rings … The burger must be eventually wrapped in newspaper and it must be eaten quickly so that the grease will not soften it till the burger sticks to the paper.[2]

Then suitably refreshed, it was time for some light entertainment. As it was still too early for the cinema, we often opted to wander across to a shopfront displaying television sets and briefly watched the latest shows screened in black and white. It was a common practice during the introduction of television into Australia towards the end on the 1950s for retailers to leave display sets turned on all night, and for small crowds to gather outside just to watch the programs. There was never any sound transmitted so it was much like watching a very old silent movie from bygone days. As we did not own a television set until 1961, it was quite a treat. Now it was time for the main act.

The Plaza Picture Theatre was an impressive old two storey building with a grandiose palatial foyer, ticketing box and regal furnishings. The ground floor level was a sea of seating bolted to timber floorboards, complete with a magnificent footboard musical organ located to one side in front of the seating and below the picture screen. This instrument served to serenade you at intermission breaks with various popular tunes played by a lady seated at the keyboard. Upstairs on the first floor landing was a different proposition, with this seating more of interest to patrons intent on throwing sweets at those seated below, or romantic couples looking for a quiet secluded location once the pictures were underway. Our family always sat on the ground floor and simply dodged the various missiles projected from above.

The opening sequences before the feature movie were always without exception current world news broadcasts, followed by a series of popular animated cartoons, such as *Heckle and Jeckle* (talking magpies), *Mighty Mouse* (mouse of tomorrow), *Popeye the Sailor* (Mr Spinach himself), *Fe-*

lix the Cat, *Casper the Friendly Ghost* and many others. On some occasions, the featurettes were accompanied by live organ music for the patrons to sing along to a tune with its words displayed on the screen and highlighted by an animated bouncing ball. There was nothing quite like a genuine communal singing session. This early part of the evening was spent consuming any sweets that I had brought with me into the theatre.

During the intermission interval before the main feature commenced, delightfully dressed usherettes wandered through the aisles on both floors, selling a comprehensive range of confectionery, nuts, ice-creams and cigarettes carried compactly in lightweight trays. This was the last opportunity to replenish your supply of Fantales (chocolate-coated caramels), Minties (mint-flavoured lollies), Marella Jubes (sugar-coated fruit jubes), Columbines (caramel toffee) or everyone's favourite Jaffas (orange-coated chocolate balls), so ideal for rolling down the aisles. For the less discerning or those with modest funds, the smaller Choo-Choo Bars (aniseed toffee), Polly Waffles (marshmallow tubes coated in chocolate) or sticky straps of licorice sufficed.

As the overhead lights slowly dimmed, the organ music sensibly ceased, the delightful usherettes evaporated from sight and the movie dramatically commenced usually with an overwhelming thunderous sound. If it was filmed in black and white, such as the gangster movie *The Trap* (1959) or the very popular western *Winchester '73* (1950), I was less than impressed. If it was filmed in colour, and in particular Technicolor, the visual effects were spectacular. Exciting western movies like *The Naked Spur* (1953) and *The Last Wagon* (1956) were some memorable examples of enriched colours, whilst many of the popular musicals of those days were always in colour, including *Oklahoma* (1955), *Carousel* (1956) and *South Pacific* (1958) in glorious stereophonic sound.

Such was the impact on Australian audiences of imported American films with the new technology of marvellous Technicolor that as early as 1952, the ratio being imported was 74 per cent American, and only 18 per cent of British films which remained associated with black and white film. Publicity posters for upcoming films from Hollywood were bigger and brighter than before, and reinforced that everything about the American film industry was glamorous, exciting and modern. The cinema could be seductive and experts feared that Hollywood movies in particular might become the model for teenage behaviour.[3]

Some films produced in Cinemascope yielded widescreen results for further dramatic effect, such as the Jules Verne live-action and cult classic *Twenty Thousand Leagues Under the Sea*, by Walt Disney Productions in which the gigantic squid attacking the submariners seemed to occupy the entire screen. Indeed, in those pre-television days, the cinema produced many magical and entrancing moments which ultimately would be replaced by a raft of alternative media in the future. With such technological advances literally occurring from movie to movie, it was still an exciting time to have gone to the cinema each week just to experience those theatrical improvements.

For most people departing the picture theatre at closing time, it was a short walk to the car-park, but for our family, it meant a very long walk home along an unlit Cranbourne Road. First we passed the Frankston cemetery and at night without any street lighting, this was always a surreal experience for me. Having recently experienced the truly scary science fiction movie *The Blob* released by Paramount Pictures in 1958 about a gelatinous alien life form that consumed everything in its path, I almost ran past the cemetery that night. This B-rated movie originally made to appeal to teenagers starred the late and great young actor Steve McQueen in his feature film debut in a lead role as the teenage hero. Next on the journey home, we encountered a disused horse trough in which I foolishly rinsed my hands still sticky from handling the licorice. In the dark, I failed to realise that the trough water was frog-infested and covered in a green algal slime. It seemed to be a night for peculiar experiences.

Eventually as we walked further from Frankston and past the local Colortone Brickworks, I realised that we were still only halfway home. Houses were quite infrequent after this point and without any street lighting we were enveloped in pitch darkness. No more cars passed us on the road at such a late hour so it was walk on and keep walking through the brisk night air. Best way to keep fit that I knew in those days. When we eventually reached home, it was straight to bed for me to anticipate the movie advertised for next Friday night when hopefully my father would want to drive into Frankston to collect us.

Figure 29: Horse trough with frogs and tadpoles (© Shutterstock)

Beaches Near and Far

There has always been a close affinity between Australians and the beach, and this was particularly the case in the 1950s. The simple pleasures were countless; from swimming in the ocean, frolicking in the surf, being dumped unceremoniously by a rogue wave, fruitlessly endeavouring to construct sand castles at the tidal edge and lying in the sun for hours, to scouring the shoreline for interesting marine shells, pieces of unusual driftwood, massive clumps of seaweed tangles, discarded objects washed up by the sea, and occasionally, retrieving lost coins from fellow beachgoers. A day at the beach was a family experience to be truly savoured. Despite living on a semi-rural property, we were still only some six kilometres driving distance from our nearest bayside beach located at Frankston, as well as being in reasonable driving proximity to further beaches stretched along the Mornington Peninsula.

The beach at Frankston was at one end of an 18 kilometre broad stretch of sand extending along the eastern coastline of Port Phillip Bay and comprised clean well-sorted beach sands formed in the last few thousand years. A second zone well past Frankston stretched a further 26 kilometres south along this coastline to the tip of the peninsula. As a result, these beaches were particularly popular with holidaymakers.[1]

The deep yellow siliceous sand at Frankston beach was remarkably clean and a well-sorted, even-grained variety, and thus relatively easily mouldable when delicately constructing a sand castle. However, to successfully build a regal edifice such as a sand castle required a prudent choice of location on the beach. If I selected the construction site close to the tidal edge, the sand was excessively moist and pliable which greatly assisted construction. Conversely, it was most likely to be a calamitous decision due the relentless wave surges or perhaps inadvertent destruction by clumsy passing beachgoers walking at the water's edge.

Selecting an isolated site on dry sand well away from the sea could result in a spectacular structure, but one that remained vulnerable and fragile due to the extreme dryness of the sand. Even refined embellishment of the completed castle with ornate sea shells never precluded it from obliteration by other children simply bent on destruction. It was simply safer to forget the castle and excavate a large hole in the wet sand, jump in and let the tide wash over you.

It was truly incredible how innovative children were in those bygone days whilst spending the entire day on the beach. Left to their own devices with not much more than a plastic spade, a small sand bucket and possibly an underwater diver's face mask, young children became instant engineers, explorers, divers, Olympic athletes and most of all, beachcombers relentlessly seeking new treasures. The beach offered that rare opportunity for children to become amphibious and discover entirely new worlds that were not possible living on the land. My memorable recollections of our local beach are both pleasant and not so pleasant.

I recall having spent an entire day on the beach once as a youngster during winter, albeit without driving rain and thunderous conditions. It was an overcast day with passing showers but so bitterly cold that it was better to stay in the sea just to remain warm. There was a dilemma to be faced – stay on the beach getting wet from passing rain showers and shivering from the cold conditions, or remain in the sea staying wet but warmer. My mother always espoused the health benefits of swimming in seawater and sincerely believed in swimming in winter. Although it was a reasonably mild day for winter, I actually enjoyed being the only one in the family perched on the rain-drenched sand, and managed to retrieve quite a collection of lost coins exposed in the sand atop of small pinnacles formed by the force of the rain. When it seemed like I had an entire beach to myself due to the inclement weather, it was truly invigorating.

On the other hand, an entire day spent on the beach during the intense heat of summer had particularly adverse outcomes for my health. Show me anyone from the 50s and 60s that has not experienced severe sunburn as a youngster, despite wearing some protective clothing, sitting under the proverbial beach umbrella for shade and taking sensible precautions, like leaving the beach before noon to avoid the heat of the day for example. Fortunately, it only happened to me once and subsequently involved a trusted household remedy of a soothing cold freshwater bath of milk and diluted vinegar solution to relieve the extreme pain of the skin burn. The lesson learned was for life and it never recurred.

One of the beach's attractions to me was the seemingly endless wooden Frankston pier, and what an iconic seafront landmark to behold. Constructed in 1857 and extended in 1864, the pier stretched for 547 yards (500 metres) and provided quite a focal point for anglers, swimmers and the public alike over the past 150 years.[2] As a youngster who only visited the local beach on occasion, I thoroughly enjoyed walking the length of this impressive structure, and was particularly taken by 'the deep end' at its extremity. There were many tales recounted by friends of massive man-eating sharks that lived around this end of the pier, attracted from the depths should anyone inadvertently fall into the sea.

I never saw anyone dive off that deep end of the pier for obvious reasons, but certainly observed many others diving along its length. On one unfortunate day whilst lying on my stomach curiously watching the fish swimming beneath the pier, one of my friends grabbed both of my ankles and shoved me over the pier edge. Hanging upside down and firmly held by one's ankles was daunting enough even without the prospect of that friend releasing me to drop helplessly into the sea below. Overwhelmed with intense trepidation that I was about to meet a shark face-to-face, I begged the friend to stop fooling around, which he duly did by pulling me back onto the pier. His reward was being promptly chased down by me along the entire length of pier until he relented and apologised profusely.

I have another most lucid recollection of a considerably smaller beach located slightly further southwards from Frankston along the Mornington Peninsula, but this was on private property in the late 50s. It was on a rare visit to a prestigious stretch of the coast and a rambling estate with a palatial cliff-top home and various small outbuildings so reminiscent of those grand architectural dwellings established around the end of the previous century. The two-storey mansion was set on landscaped cliff tops overlooking the bay, within spacious grounds of beautiful gardens and meticulously manicured lawns.

I was able to negotiate the steep steps cut into the outcropping rock at the rear of the estate to reach the isolated pocket of beach perched below, tightly squeezed against the base of the adjacent towering vertical cliffs. This tranquil seaside sanctuary offered a narrow strip of deep yellow sand deposited in a small surrounding cove that was only accessible either from the property's rock-steps etched out of the cliff face above, or perhaps by using the solitary rowboat left on the beach. Such a vision of an idyllic and secluded private beach remained with me for years after that unique visit, and must have been such a relaxing venue for the home's owners.

If the family budget was sufficient for an annual summer holiday, it was usual to travel about 55 kilometres to the extreme tip of the Mornington Peninsula in Port Phillip Bay, or even as far as beaches located some 200 kilometres away westwards along the Great Ocean Road that abutted Bass Strait. For such a youngster, these were massive distances travelled and new locations to be explored. The effort was always worthwhile and provided immense opportunities to experience the wild untamed surf conditions of the ocean and all its inherent hazards, as well as great beachcombing times.

Sorrento's Ocean Beach at the narrow end of the Peninsula faced Bass Strait, whereas its Front Beach on the opposite side nestled beside the relatively calmer waters of Port Phillip Bay. Ocean Beach was untamed, brutal and experienced the full brunt of any passing inclement weather often with surging tides, massive clumps of tangled and ropey kelp beds and treacherous undercurrents. It was invigorating and strenuous. At least once whilst swimming with the family, I became hopelessly entangled within the intertwined mess of kelp seaweed that more resembled immense layers of elongated strips than weed. With each tidal surge, it was difficult to remain unattached from the clutches of those underwater forests. Consequently, it was often necessary for the family to alternate between the twin beaches, if not just to get a quiet swim in calmer waters, and to recuperate for the next day's battle with that other wild beach.

Not far from Sorrento was the lonely wind-swept beach at Portsea, considerably nearer to the extreme tip of the Peninsula. This beach had two exceptional attractions. My favourite was the public sea bath constructed in the natural coastal rock in which you safely swam isolated from treacherous currents and without fear of being washed away. However, on days of particularly rough sea conditions, every so often a gigantic wave broke over the rock barrier and submerged me in a thunderous shower of seawater.

If I was vigilant and observed the oncoming behemoth, it was possible to dive underwater before it crashed down on the sea bath. If perhaps my back was turned to the ocean, it was a deluge of water, foam and often seaweed raining from the heavens. The other attraction of this beach was that it was exposed to the extreme elements of Bass Strait. However, it was probably far more precarious to swim here than at Sorrento, as seaweed beds of ropey kelp were everywhere. As a consequence, our family preferred the nearby public sea bath, and on rare calm days when the howling winds had abated, that rock pool was sheer bliss.

Expeditions further afield were along the Great Ocean Road on Victoria's south-western coastline with Bass Strait, and usually ended on a beach with tremendous appeal to those seeking the wide open spaces. For an avid young beachcomber like myself, walking the endless beach and scouring the various high tide marks for interesting objects was paradise. One did not need to venture more than a few metres before something partially buried in sand attracted your notice – an object, perhaps shiny, of peculiar shape or colour, or just extraordinary. There was always a diverse array of sea shells and marine creatures, such as small crabs, jelly fish and the odd cuttlefish left along these tide lines, but every so often, there was also something extra special. It may be a fancy starfish, a miniscule mortified sea horse or an enormous shell washed up from the oceanic depths, but they all represented small treasures to me.

The peculiar range of manufactured objects discarded by the retreating tides never ceased to amuse me on these solitary beach escapades; metal bottle caps, glass bottles of every size, coloured glass fragments worn into weird shapes by relentless currents and wave action, planks, timber honeycombed and rounded at the edges, the occasional life jacket, sandals, worn toothbrushes, further paraphernalia of human existence, fish netting, buoys, and other miscellaneous nautical items. Plastics and the myriad of disposable products so prevalent in today's society were most uncommon in those times. Often I wandered the long stretches of beach for hours as time had no bearing when exploring. My mother once casually remarked that she sometimes thought that I had reached China in my travels as I was gone for so long. Of all my collectibles gathered along that beach, only a few precious oddments ever returned home with me, and probably that was important because there was always next year's expedition.

The magic of staying for a week or more in such a tranquil location was the result of renting an entirely self-contained holiday cottage virtually on the foreshore. The cost was extremely modest, the facilities comfortable and spacious, and with other young families doing likewise, it was easy to make childhood friends. A few days after our arrival, I joined the group of my new acquaintances who had congregated on the beach following breakfast, and set off to explore the endless tracts of sand dunes and scrutinise whatever the tide may have delivered overnight. Many enjoyable hours were spent as intrepid adventurers or simply savouring the local surf. Such areas were rarely crowded with holiday-makers, thus permitting unbridled freedom to roam the beach.

When I enjoyed the ocean as a youngster, it always stirred the mariner in me, and what was a mariner without a ship? For this sea adventurer, my ship was a meticulously hand-crafted, wooden model schooner complete with keel, rudder, realistic cloth sails, portholes, shiny brass fittings and beautifully painted with a bright blue hull and a golden trim. It was the best Christmas present ever for a young seafarer about to embark on his next voyage of discovery along the Great Ocean Road. I launched the schooner in the beach shallows with full sails set and watched with delight as it took the breeze and sailed on. The vessel was an exact model of the full size version and a miniature miracle of engineering design. When the breeze faltered, the vessel languished and so did I. Kept that schooner forever and valued the craftsmanship in its intricate detail. Avast ye landlubbers, it be young Capt'n King on the high seas.

Figure 30: My famous schooner

No beach holiday would be complete without the family umbrella to provide essential shade protection from the searing sun. Our family always had a multi-coloured, striped beach umbrella with a staunch wooden pole buried deep into the sand to minimise it blowing away. Of course, even a reasonably strong gust of wind always dislodged the umbrella, relentlessly rolling and spinning it wildly across the sand for a short distance only to be retrieved and quickly reinstated. This item became such a family necessity over many years, that even in my adulthood whilst raising my own family, I always took a beach umbrella whenever we visited the beach. Strange how such a habit that formed in my earliest childhood stayed with me forever.

The concept of having a sanctuary of permanent shade available on the beach to shelter from the scorching sun was clever. After swimming, our family quickly gathered beneath the umbrella jostling for any available shade and for temporary relief from the burning sand. Lunch was always served under this all-day retreat. I am unsure why sandwiches always tasted better at the beach but our lunches were memorable for their range of sandwich fillings. It was a lucky dip ranging from ham with pickles, curried egg, more ham (perhaps this time with salad), to cheese and tomato, chicken and tomato, and corned beef on occasion. Messy wet beetroot was never included in our sandwiches for obvious reasons.

For refreshment, lemonade was a mandatory replenishment for the children, and was usually served lukewarm without the benefit of any ice. It still tasted great anyway. Afterwards, it was playing on the sand for about an hour until lunch had been properly digested and then a sprint straight back into the ocean. Even after spending the entire day on the beach, it only ever felt like a few hours to me, and before I realised, it was time to leave. There was always tomorrow to do it all over again.

In the early 60s, there were two essential beach toys for children to fully enjoy any day's activities. The first was a homemade thin plywood and rounded skiffle board 24 inches (600mm) in diameter and one half inch (10mm) in thickness. These skimming boards were dropped into the shallow wash of previous waves remaining at the water's edge along a shoreline, and then ridden along the top of this thin layer of water at speed. There were two techniques to perfect successful skimming over the water; leave the board stationary and jump onto to it at a fast pace, thereby using my own momentum to travel, or stand on the skim board with one leg and use the other leg to propel myself along. The first technique usually resulted in me overturning unceremoniously, and the second technique was hard work gaining enough momentum and so resulted more in a skidding/jolting ride than a skimming manoeuvre.

The other beach toy was my favourite and needed to be hired by the hour at concession stands located along the beach during holiday periods. It was an inflatable surf mat or 'floatie' made of heavy duty and durable canvas, complete with thin cord/rope threaded along each side and at one end for gripping the mat whilst in surf. For children like me, the recommended size was 45 inches long x 29 inches wide (1.14m x 0.74m), although there was also a larger mat available for adults of 60 inches (1.52m) in length. Given that I only had an hour to master a technique of surviving in breaking surf and had to share the surf mat with my older sister as well, timing was critical.

I quickly learned to adjust my speed in the waves by holding onto the front corners of the mat, but underestimated the sheer power of a few waves as well. This resulted in the mat folding away underneath me whilst riding the bigger waves and my body being projected like a missile down the front of the wave, only to have the same wave then crash upon me, just as a final indignity. Dragging myself to shore in a bedraggled state and minus the surf mat, I turned to see my sister gleefully retrieve the offending mat and swim straight back into the turbulent surf on it. Despondent about my failure, I tried again when it was eventually my turn but unfortunately again selected a gigantic wave beyond my limited abilities. This time, I managed to remain on the surf mat as the wave crashed to earth, but the resultant up-swell impact sent both me and the mat yet again flying in separate directions.

As I dragged myself to the shoreline to the raucous laughter and applause of some onlookers, I wondered what all the fuss was about until I noticed my bathers had filled to capacity with wet sand and my hair was strewn with seaweed. I must have looked quite a sight emerging from the raging surf, much like some bewildered sea beast cast out of the deep in a fierce storm. If this was fun, then perhaps I should have stayed home. Fortunately, my mother had brought the Mercurochrome to the beach to apply to those abundant skin cuts and abrasions that I had incurred. After that medical treatment and the extensive staining of my skin by the antiseptic, I definitely needed a rest. As a final humiliation, I noticed that my sister had quickly perfected the technique of surf mat riding without ever being dumped by a wave and was thoroughly enjoying herself in the surf.

My other enduring recollection about the beach was swimwear. It was before the introduction of skimpy bikinis and women tended to wear single piece bathers and most wore a swim cap to protect their hair from the ravages of the ocean's salt water. In the 1950s, caps were made of heavy latex rubber, as well as being cumbersome and tight to wear, but were essential to protect a lady's expensive hairstyle. My sister always wore a plain coloured swimming cap out of necessity, but my mother preferred the more fashionable flower petal decorated caps. It did not really matter either way as trying to remove them without scalping oneself was extremely difficult, and latex rubber had a habit of clinging to your hair until the very last moment. I never considered the beach to be an important place to exhibit fashionable swimwear so was quite content with my Speedo shorts, now widely acknowledged as retro-style bathers.

Mornington Peninsula and more

The Mornington Peninsula had almost always been a popular destination for holiday makers and day trippers from the city intent on enjoying the delights and natural wonders of the local coastal areas. Although camping in tents, sometimes residing in caravans or taking a holiday cottage was common in the late 50s, there was a sprinkling of holiday camps wisely constructed in proximity to the foreshore. We only ever stayed in one at Rye, located almost at the end of the Peninsula. Its accommodation was basic yet comfortable and most importantly, located only a short walking distance from nearby Port Phillip Bay.

What I always recall about these camps were the diverse recreational facilities for youngsters that were usually established in common halls. Table tennis was one of the most popular pursuits, followed closely by indoor and outdoor amenities for playing various other ball games. I recall these camps having spacious grounds, providing plenty of options to go exploring around the local neighbourhood without ever leaving the rambling property. There was also a distinctive emphasis on simply enjoying the natural environment, with much of the camp retaining the native vegetation of the area.

It may not have been as elaborate as today, but these community camps provided a sensible range of equipment and play spaces to keep children occupied through the summer school holiday period, combined with seashore visits. I suppose most of the enjoyment was in meeting other children and quickly developing friendships, albeit only for a week. By the end of the holiday, we were all part of one group or another, and after breakfast tended to do everything together for a day's activities, leaving the parents to their own devices.

The Mornington Peninsula was still largely undeveloped forests interspersed between a splattering of small agricultural farms, spacious fruit orchards, and a diversity of various primary producers (particularly livestock), with the exception of a narrow coastal fringe of residential and tourism development. Any formal planning scheme by the Mornington Shire to urbanise the Peninsula would not be finalised until the end of the 1950s, when it was thought to be the first rural local government in Victoria to adopt such a scheme across its entire extent.[1]

The Peninsula always had been a place for recreational and leisure pursuits, and given the plethora of charming beaches, the picturesque beauty of the coastline and a profusion of natural environment wonders that abounded inland, it was little wonder that the description as 'Melbourne's playground' was embraced by so many. A day trip for our family in our old Chrysler automobile was always an adventure and we never quite knew where we would finish our journey. I recall thickly wooded forests that grew so prolifically on both sides of the road that there was no sunlight penetrating the combined canopy, and narrow roads suitable only for a single vehicle where a driver had to almost pull off the road to permit an oncoming vehicle to safely pass. Such outings always included a packed picnic lunch and much travelling to see special locales as was customary in those days.

Foxey's Hangout was one such extraordinary location of public curiosity, and was truly worth the journey. It involved a tale of eradication of vermin foxes in the local farming neighbourhood and the daily rivalry that arose between two bounty hunters. Foxey's Hangout had been a recognisable site for displaying the vermin as trophies since the late 1930s, and indicated the intense but friendly competitive spirit that eventuated between the two local fox trappers. Most importantly, it was a place signifying that eradication of an introduced vermin was successful, albeit graphically displayed by hanging the dead foxes from every accessible branch.

When we finally located that large conspicuous eucalyptus tree on the junction of two rural roads where the scoundrels were displayed, it was both memorable and absorbing. The many branches were littered with dead foxes that so clearly indicated to me how much of a plague they must have been to the local landholders. After the eventual deaths of both trappers, friends and neighbours were believed to have eventually revived the custom and maintained the practice for many years. Of course that tree is now long dead and in 2011, the remaining tree trunk was relocated to the side of the road to signify the location. A nearby minor road also has the relevant title of Foxey's Road. Foxes by their very nature are incredibly cautious and cunning foes, avoiding capture relentlessly. Trappers remain an important ingredient in the sensible mix to remove this introduced species from decimating both Australia's precious dwindling native fauna and valuable domestic livestock.

The woodland forests passed on our road trips were most memorable, and given the timber felling and clearing that probably occurred as more and more areas became urbanised, I doubt that many of those tracts still remain today other than in protected natural reserves. Early Shire maps of the Peninsula in the first years of white settlement revealed '… extensive forested areas where Eucalyptus and Stringybark grew profusely…' and in the mid-1800s, '… A survey of the coastal portions of the district… noted undulating grassy plains timbered with she-oak and wattle…'[2]

My recollections of the late 50s were of passing many magnificent stands of eucalyptus trees of massive height and density as we travelled through these areas, sometimes stopping for a picnic lunch on the side of the road without even seeing another vehicle pass by. When travelling off the main roads, perhaps following a rural cross road, I recalled feeling as if you were truly in the bush, and not a mere few miles from urban areas.

These backroads were quiet and secluded with barely any traffic. Sometimes, we stopped to purchase fresh fruit and vegetables from an unmanned stall erected at the end of a farmer's driveway, and left the correct amount of money for the purchase. Such was the honesty of those days. I also recall the vibrant and diverse birdlife in those densely forested areas, probably only experienced today in protected bird sanctuaries. During our roadside picnics, it was a delight to listen to the cacophony of shrill and raucous bird sounds as the various species competed to be heard in the forest. Above all else, I remember how the air was so clean and fresh amongst this vegetation, almost to the point of being intoxicating.

On one special occasion, our family stopped in a spectacular grove of golden yellow Cootamundra wattle trees in full blossom that were growing freely along the sides of that rural road. We decided not to picnic there as the slightest breeze scattered the masses of accumulated fallen blossoms in the air and all over us. It was also common to encounter various wildlife, such as kangaroos and wallabies placidly sitting beside the road verges before bounding away as our car approached. I suppose as vehicles only travelled these backroads infrequently, that native wildlife were relatively cautious of automobiles.

Tea rooms were very popular for a stop-over during road trips through the Mornington Peninsula. I cannot recall their names or locations due to my young age at the time, but have always remembered the fresh homemade scones with whipped cream and strawberry jam served with each order. The compact tables each had a fancy lace tablecloth and were spacious enough for two adults and perhaps two smaller children to be seated. Tea was brewed and served from a porcelain teapot into cups with saucers, and there was always a choice of scones, cake or small quarter sandwiches with special fillings. The tea rooms usually had an outdoor area or verandah where it was possible to enjoy the sights and sounds of the forest whilst taking our repast and if we were fortunate, local birdlife might even venture close to the dining area seeking to sample some of our scones or cake.

Another special time of the year for me was attending the Wharfie's annual community picnic and it was surely a day like no other for a young child. It was held predominantly for the enjoyment of families and other relatives of current and past 'wharfies' (also known as dock labourers, lumpers or stevedores). This event was not unlike the song about the mythical Teddy Bears' Picnic of folklore that is so well known to many:

> ...See them gaily gad about
> They love to play and shout
> They never have any cares...
> ...Every Teddy Bear who's been good
> Is sure of a treat today

There's lots of marvellous things to eat
And wonderful games to play
Beneath the trees where nobody sees
They'll hide and seek as long as they please...[3]

The picnic was particularly for children and typically held on a Sunday in Frankston not too distant from the foreshore. My father had been a wharf labourer on the docks of Sydney during the terrible Great Depression of the 1930s, and fully valued his work, given so many others were unemployed. Later, he worked at the Port Melbourne docks in Victoria and endured extremely harsh conditions of manual labour where much shipping cargo from drums and crates to bales and piles of lumber were still transported/lumped by hand. This annual picnic day was a rare opportunity to reward such men for their arduous efforts and provide something special for their families.

Imagine a day where no expense whatsoever was spared catering for families, and a day for all to remember. Everything was free and in abundant supply, from fresh hot dogs to ice-cream in wafer cones, from fairy floss to soft drinks, and more still. All you had to do was consume it. There were cursory athletic events such as sprints in which every competitor was awarded a prize, and impromptu group events just for the sheer fun of it. Sack races were held using old oversized hessian bags that were so large the children competing kept falling over or colliding with each other and nobody even reached the finish line.

The picnic lunch included endless cold and hot meats, incredible salads and fresh bread loaves followed by more ice cream, jellies, tarts and cakes. As the day drew to a close, there was still one more totally unexpected surprise left for the children. Each and every child received a small white paper bag crammed to overflowing with lollies, supplemented with a bottle of icy-cold soft drink. The sweets were a great combination of toffees, caramels, musk stix, licorice allsorts and straps, and a few others that I cannot recall – every child's dream and every dentist's nightmare.

Someone had gone to considerable effort to ensure the choice of lollies rather than the amount was satisfying. I recall even receiving a bottle of creamy soda one year as our family left, and if you are old enough to remember that flavour, then you are probably too old by now. I always preferred raspberry-flavoured soft drink (also known as 'crimson' flavour) despite it leaving your lips stained red afterwards. Such were the sacrifices that a youngster made in those halcyon days.

Whilst on the subject of my childhood travels, I must include annual pilgrimages outside of the State. I became accustomed to travelling interstate to New South Wales from an early age, when my mother took me on the Spirit of Progress train from Melbourne to Albury on the Victorian border, and thence to Sydney on the connecting overnighter train. It may have only been a rail journey between capital cities over one night, but certainly was the longest trip for me. We typically only purchased modest seated accommodation rather than sleeper cabins, and tried to catch some sleep over the 12 hour night journey.

This was difficult due to frequent stops at numerous stations, transferring entirely between trains near midnight due to different rail gauges between the two States, and the incessant disturbances of other passengers not choosing to sleep. What an entirely new world presented to me once in Sydney. Brightly coloured, red double-decker buses exactly like British buses, ferries across the famous harbour and an underground rail system were enlightening. However, there were no electric trams and the city streets were very narrow compared to Melbourne.

Much of my interstate time was spent in suburbia with my grandmother and her neighbour known as 'Aunty Clara' who resided on the opposite side of the street. Aunty Clara was a horse racing fanatic, and through her mentoring, taught me everything there was to know about the sport of kings. By scrupulous studying of a horse's pedigree and previous performances over various distances, the horse's starting weight, the race barrier position, the jockey, the condition of the race track and weather, I was able to accurately gauge if a horse would be successful. It was after all, simply a hobby.

As a pastime we attended mid-week and Saturday race meetings at Randwick, Canterbury and Rose Hill, keeping any unsuccessful betting tickets and the racetrack's form pocket book as souvenirs. By the time I was around 11 or 12 years of age and relatively tall for my age, it was not uncommon for fellow race-goers to commonly mistake me for a young apprentice jockey.

Of course, I was far too young to engage in horse race betting, but my selections were often chosen by my mother as a definite prospect. My worst regret was a horse named Grecian Vale who ran in the very last race of the day and was considered no chance whatsoever to win, with virtually no prior performance history. My mother ignored my advice and neglected to place the minimum five shilling (50 cents) bet to win on that horse. It won the race and paid a handsome princely dividend of £200 ($400) for such a modest outlay. In today's equivalent value, this would have represented a windfall of almost $5600 in 2016.[4] Upon returning home after our day out, the early evening was typically spent watching the televised replay of every race and comparing all betting tickets in case there had been any successes missed in the day's activities.

One other event remains steadfastly retained in my memories from those racetrack visits, and that was of a lady unknown to us who won an enormous amount of money on a single bet. This stranger was collecting her winnings in the queue just in front of us and was so overcome with joy, she generously gave the operator of the betting stall a £5 note ($10). She then turned to the person standing behind her and handed them several one pound notes before quickly walking away and indiscriminately casting £1 notes wildly into the air. Naturally, this started a minor scuffle between other patrons desperately lunging at the airborne currency. The stranger disappeared into the surging crowd still tightly gripping the huge wad of remaining notes and we did not see her again. Such was the effect of a substantial win at the races.

There were many subtle differences to me between Sydney and Melbourne, including Streets (ultra-creamy) ice-cream, Aeroplane Jelly (for the memorable advertising jingle and delicious flavours), Shelley's lemonade, ginger beer, pineapple and creaming soda, and any Schweppes soft drink (with real fruit pieces) to name but a few of my childhood interests. More importantly however, colourful vans passed through your street each afternoon selling soft serve ice-cream and playing catchy musical tunes. It was far more than a tradition to purchase such ice-cream in a delectable wafer cone, it was mandatory.

People's habits were certainly different. When my mother decided to paint my grandmother's weathered white picket front fence at 11 pm at night to avoid too many spectators, she actually attracted a small group of onlookers in the quiet suburban street who politely complimented her on her artistic prowess.

Trapdoor spiders were unheard of in Melbourne but prolific throughout the backyard of my grandmother's property. Although they resembled the more dangerous funnel-web spiders also found in Sydney, they were not venomous and relatively timid unless threatened. As a precaution, my grandmother purchased a small wooden pop-gun toy rifle for me, complete with a tiny cork attached to a length of string as the projectile. I spent many enjoyable hours improving my accuracy with that little pop-gun in case of a sneak attack from those trapdoor spiders.

The remainder of my annual visits to New South Wales in the 50s to mid-60s were spent on the south coast near Wollongong where more relatives resided. Travelling by rail in coal-fired steam trains that slowly passed through innumerable tunnels and beside that spectacular coastline was exhilarating and quite an adventure. The journey probably lasted around two hours and stopped at over twenty railway stations en route. Swimming in the ocean along this south coast was also vastly different to the beaches near home. Long flat wave-cut platforms underlying the coastal sands meant you walked out from the beach at about waist height for at least one hundred metres before encountering any deep water, and oncoming waves would roll-in considerable distances before you finally reached the deep. On days of rough sea conditions, this meant fighting a series of consecutive waves crashing into you in waters too shallow to dive beneath without striking your head on the sandy ocean floor.

On one particularly freezing winter's morning at 7 am when even the two lifeguards on duty were wearing heavy woollen overcoats and wool beanies on their heads, our little family group bravely ventured into the sea at

Corrimal near Wollongong. To describe the seawater temperature as arctic was probably an exaggeration, but when combined with a strong prevailing onshore wind and serious waves, it was still quite challenging. Then miraculously, once you were in the turbulent wash of seawater, foam and crashing waves, it was invigorating.

The bitter cold evaporated and being in the ocean tolerable, until you left the water to scurry across the beach, much to the accompanying merriment of those lifeguards. Then it rained and combined with that chilly wind to send us back into the raging surf merely to stay warm. It may be difficult for some to appreciate swimming in the wild surf on a freezing winter's day, but our family always loved going to the beach regardless of the weather. It was a healthy pastime combined with battling nature's elements of wind, rain and surf. One of life's simplest pleasures to me and provided great memories.

Even though we stayed with my mother's relatives during these visits to New South Wales, they rarely went to the beach, and I think missed out on an incredible natural attraction. They never visited us in Victoria, perhaps due the distances involved travelling interstate, and we only ever saw them every couple of years, although it was always exciting for me.

Collectibles and other Interests

As my father travelled extensively in his early years before starting our family, he had amassed collectibles from throughout the world out of personal interest. There was a diverse range of oddments at home amongst some special items, which for a young child, were simply fascinating. From time to time, I enjoyed rummaging through these souvenirs and exotic artefacts just to examine them in more detail and perhaps uncover some treasures. It was probably the stimulus for me to commence my own journey. Literary works were particularly of interest to me.

Where does one start in describing the incredibly rich diversity of collectibles that children in that golden era actively acquired, both as play/leisure items and for trading to like-minded individuals. Before the mass saturation of domestic households in Australia with black and white television sets, literary cultivation of the mind by book reading was supreme. All children owned hardcover glossy books usually encompassing adventure stories, science fiction tales, western (Cowboys and Indians) legends, romantic tales, fairy tales or drama stories, commonly with suitable illustrations and images. Often these relatively expensive books were combinations of themes and of considerable interest as a result.

There were dramatic nautical tales of buccaneers on the Spanish Main engaged in deadly sea battles between ships firing canon after canon, of pirates and treacherous brigands swarming over the decks of some unsuspecting merchant vessel and raising the Skull and Crossbones flag, or of treasure chests overflowing with gold doubloons and exotic jewellery secretly buried on an obscure mysterious island. Meticulously detailed and colourful illustrations of these characters and their adventures embellished the stories and provided realism to such rollicking yarns.

Science fiction hardcover books were usually only in illustration format, often depicting futuristic worlds beyond the imagination. Armies of Troks (robots with rounded shapes) and Grebs (robots resembling rectangular boxes on wheels) incessantly waged war between each other, and anyone else visiting their planet. Of course for those seeking strictly literary satisfaction, a plethora of monthly science fiction and futuristic science magazines including science fantasy abounded with catchy titles, such as *Imagination, Amazing Stories, Fantastic Universe, Astounding Science Fiction, New Worlds or The Magazine of Fantasy & Science Fiction.*

By the late 1950s, space travel was becoming a reality as unmanned rockets were successfully launched and the first spacecraft transported an animal (*Laika* the dog) into orbit by the end of 1957. Many youngsters dreamed of becoming astronauts and their monthly magazines provided a wealth of imaginative tales about space travel to distant galaxies. These magazines also explored other possible lifeforms in the universe, and in some respects, reinforced the mass popularity of science fiction movies at the cinema.

Westerns were extremely popular in hardcover books about the 'Old West', ranging from legendary yarns about gunfighters like Billy the Kid and Wild Bill Hickok, outlaw gangs like the Daltons and the Clantons, feared lawmen like the Earp Brothers and Pat Garrett, to pioneering frontiersmen like Davey Crockett and Daniel Boone. When boys were not dreaming about space travel, it was time to strap on your cowboy holster and practice becoming the fastest cap-gun in town. *Little Golden Books of Children's Classics* were another highly fancied and diverse source of beautifully illustrated stories, including folktales, fables, nursery rhymes and legendary tales from the past, as well as about nature and science. Immaculately presented in a compact series of hardcover gold edged books, these educational and entertaining stories were almost mandatory in our popular culture for young folk wishing to learn.

Comic books were probably far more compulsive reading material for such youngsters, albeit of a less serious nature. Comics were comparatively cheaper to purchase than hardcover books and readily available to children in many outlets, including every newsagency and even from variety stores (now largely supermarkets). The sheer choice in the marketplace was overwhelming and required discipline to contain one's expenditure. After all, some comics were never worth trading to other children unless of superior quality.

The high quality upmarket *Classics Illustrated* comics were amongst the superior collectibles for any youngster, with engaging titles such as *The Master Of Ballantrae, Ivanhoe, Moby Dick* and *The Three Musketeers*. The list of comic titles available through those bygone days would fill a book today, and certainly my personal collection filled at least one cupboard. They were stacked in multiple layers in newsagencies, much like magazines nowadays, and many a child would browse through the selection before purchasing.

By 1952, it was estimated that Australians purchased 60 million comic books annually, with most imported from the US.[1] Similar to cinema movies from Hollywood in the 50s, '... the imported American comic book now appeared in large numbers. Sales rocketed and by 1954, 60 million comics were sold annually'.[2] To gauge the enormous impact of such volumes, consider that most avid comic readers were probably aged between 7 and 15 years of age and in 1954, there were only 1.35 million children within that entire age group in this country.[3] It suggests children were buying many comics in those times.

This trend was only offset to a very minor extent by the immense admiration of comic strips published in a full page of Australia's various daily newspapers, such as *Ginger Meggs, The Potts, Pop, Dick Tracey, The Phantom, Saltbush Bill* and *Blondie*. It was common to track the adventures of these serial comic strips from day to day just to enjoy the eventual outcomes. Although the introduction of television in the late 50s was to ultimately provide serious entertainment alternatives to the humble comic, this was not the case in our household. Regrettably, in later years of life, my own treasured comic books were probably sold for a mere pittance at weekend Trash and Treasure Markets convened in Frankston, rather than retained into adulthood.

Of the innumerable precious collectibles actively sought in the 1950s and beyond, young people thrived on amassing postage stamp collections and collecting swap cards contained in various packaged commercial products, such as chocolate bars, packets of tea and even breakfast cereals. Stamp collecting was more than simply a hobby, it was a bona fide obsession. Novice philatelists always had a large multi-page stamp album complete with pre-arranged mounting sleeves to carefully store and protect each stamp, and a special pair of handling tweezers to preclude damaging the items.

The reward was in locating and keeping every stamp that you could possibly find, as in those days, people communicated predominantly by mailed letters always requiring at least one postage stamp. Even neighbours and school friends were recruited to retain their used postage stamps and donate them to my collection. Any overseas mail received was treated as a bonanza, particularly from distant places, such as the United Kingdom, Europe and Asia. Occasionally, this bonanza became a real treasure if the postage stamp was rare, expensive, exotic or most importantly, arrived in pristine condition without any marking from the postal service.

Why was this hobby so popular at the time? I surmise the attraction of collecting these miniature pictures from all over the world was not only challenging for a youngster, but educational in appreciating various cultures. I never knew what to expect when letters arrived from faraway places like Canada, United Kingdom and USA. It taught me to value such prizes both for their artistic content and their symbolic message. The hobby was a long term exercise over years and grew proportionately to the letters received from within Victoria, from interstate and overseas. I eventually collected substantial and varied stamps to almost fill the album before my interest waned in older childhood. By that time, the collection contained several rare and exotic prizes, with enough additional new stamps to start a second album.

However, as was usually the case when a boy became a teenager and interests changed, the album remained stored away for years at home – secured amongst other childhood items but largely forgotten. As an adult, my interest was piqued once more but I was unable to locate the album, and presumably it met the same fate as my comics at a local Trash and Treasure market.

Swap cards were nowhere near as valuable but far easier to accumulate. Tuckfields 'Ty-nee Tips' Tea originally came in ½ lb (225 gram) packets along with a high quality laminated and coloured card depicting Australiana birds. A new larger one pound (450 gram) family pack followed in 1965. *The Birds* was an extraordinarily large and complex set of 480 trade cards that were progressively issued from 1959 over five successive series of 96 cards. One had to consume immense volumes of tea to successfully collect the entire massive set, but that was of no concern to me.

Tuckfields Teas even thoughtfully produced elaborately designed bird card albums to suit. The cards were exquisitely presented with descriptive text about each bird and often relevant naturalistic or native habitat background settings. From boobooks, budgerigars and babblers to warblers, wagtails and whipbirds, the list was virtually endless, representing a staggering 441 species that satisfied even the most avid collector It was a unique way to learn much more about our region's birdlife than by most other means, and a definitive guide for amateur bird-watchers. Tuckfields Teas also produced trade card sets of fish, dogs, cats, animals, wildflowers and Australian Heritage, but none surpassed the size of the set issued for bird cards.[4]

I suggest that one of the greatest hobbies for a young boy in the 1950s probably always involved aeroplanes, and there were three sure ways to feed this hobby. The cheapest and cleverest method was to collect colourful pictorial cards of aircraft of the world found inside Nestlé's Classic 1.45 ounce (35 gram) milk chocolate bars, thus also providing the necessary excuse to consume more of the delicacy. Nestlé chocolate was probably not as popular as Australia's favourite local producer Cadbury, perhaps because it had a distinctly different flavour. The chocolate appeared extremely dark in colouration and particularly rich in flavour, almost akin to Swiss dark chocolate.

The ruby red wrapping with regal golden lettering always distinguished the Nestlé confectionery from its competitors, as well as the small one-person size of the bar. Although I enjoyed consuming those bars, it remained an acquired taste for me, as I really purchased them for their cards. An elaborate glossy hardcover album detailing every aircraft's details and history was also available to complete the collection, although this required purchasing the block-size Nestlé milk chocolate to obtain the substantially larger selective cards required in the album. As with my other collectible albums, this disappeared at a local swap market many years later.

The second way to enjoy aircraft was to build a realistic replica model yourself from lightweight balsa wood. These kits were extremely popular and affordable, came with thorough instructions in English, and all parts were scrupulously numbered. Even the tube of special adhesive compound was included for securing the components. Half of the enjoyment was in the fastidious assembling of the aircraft. I chose a two-seater, single-engine, overhead wing light aircraft, propelled by winding its plastic propeller anti-clockwise until the attached rubber band was tightly twisted. By holding the propeller firmly between your fingers, the aircraft above your head and releasing it skyward with a gentle thrust in an open area, the replica's propeller would burst into life and send the aircraft whirring off into the distance.

Dependent upon prevailing wind conditions at the time, it flew onwards without deviation, or just followed the wind direction. Sometimes the aircraft crashed almost immediately whilst at other times, it performed all types of manoeuvres unassisted. Every day was a totally different experience and repairs were never onerous. The little plane eventually met its demise when it flew into a campfire and was consumed by the flames in a spectacular display of aerodynamics. Another way of constructing model aircraft was by purchasing the kit as plastic pre-moulded parts that were then assembled, glued together and hand-painted for appearance purposes only. Those substantially smaller models of various fighting aircraft sat on a shelf and gathered dust once completed. The enjoyment was strictly in the assembly process.

The third way to satisfy your hobby was also the most expensive. It required very prudent purchasing of the hugely successful, die-cast metal, miniature scaled models, known as the Lesney Matchbox series of toys.

Every boy in the 1950s collected these icons of the toy kingdom. They were sold in tastefully decorated, individually numbered, miniature imitation matchboxes, and were meticulous in their engineering detail. My favourites were actually vehicles such as the sports cars, luxury convertibles, tip-trucks and fire engines, but there were so many others to choose that it was a lifetime occupation of collecting.

The boom period for this vast range of highly collectible toys started in the early 1960s when its popularity in Australia became so great that the country '… had a bigger selection from the Matchbox range than anywhere else. In fact, it was Broken Hill zinc exported to the United Kingdom that the five million Matchbox cars being produced a week in 1969 were made from'.[5]

Sometimes the collecting hobby was only a matter of opening your new box of breakfast cereal and retrieving the complimentary plastic colourful figurines of Wild West Cowboys and Indians, Confederate and Union soldiers or World War 2 soldiers in various poses.

Figure 31: Wild West cowboys and indians (Kelloggs, circa 1950s - 1960s)

If you were a serious collector, such figurines and accessories were purchased as groups in entire armies, tribes or troops from the local toy hobby shops that have mostly closed today. By amassing sufficient numbers, you were able to recreate various historical battles and wars in a miniature layout, and let your imagination take over. The demise in popularity of collecting an assortment of fascinating objects by the 1960s probably arose from the introduction of television and eventually computers, and a vastly improved access to alternative forms of leisure and entertainment.

The more expensive hobbies such as intricate electric Hornby model train sets, slot racing cars and, Meccano construction sets for erecting elaborate and versatile metal engineering structures from reusable metal parts and high quality plastic parts, were always outside of my financial means. I preferred to pursue more realistic options, like printing weekly news-sheets for our local neighbourhood. I called them 'my passing interests'.

Having acquired a printer's small toy stamping press, coloured ink supply and associated collection of rubber letters, numerals and various symbols, I was keen to try my hand at compiling a local news-sheet. Armed with valuable interesting feedback from friends on local events and the weekend results from local sports' clubs, I composited the information manually and carefully printed the information a few words at a time. After adding a cartoon or joke for additional merit, I distributed my inaugural issue free to a few nearby houses, with a resultant positive response. The following week, the dual sided news-sheet was painstakingly produced at the modest issue price of one shilling (10 cents) to cover operating expenses. My labour was not included as it was a hobby after all. The news-sheet eventually faltered after only about a month due to the intensity of producing a printed document manually. My short-lived hobby as a budding journalist was over.

Our family never owned a horse in a time when plenty of other families did have one or more. Langwarrin even had a Horse and Pony Club in the 50s, renamed Langwarrin Pony Club about 1963. I had always wanted to at least learn to ride a horse or pony whilst a youngster. As it happened, a visit to the Royal Melbourne Zoological Gardens provided me with the rarest of opportunities to actually ride atop an elephant as a young zoo visitor. Such rides were something of an unusual attraction in those days and performed under strict supervision to provide a suitable zoo experience. To sit perched high above the ground on such an enormous animal was breathtaking, even as it strolled along at a leisurely pace. When I did eventually ride a horse in later years, it was a breeze compared to an elephant, and nowhere near as far from the ground.

Hand-knitting of various woollen garments was usually undertaken by my mother at various times, not only out of necessity to provide the family with additional winter clothing, but also because it was a particularly popular leisure activity prior to the distractive introduction of television. Balls of knitting wool were also readily available in diverse colours and at affordable prices. She taught me to knit, and for a while as a youngster I thoroughly embraced the pastime. I do not think that I ever completed a pullover, cardigan or scarf, but it was fun trying. My sister was always faster and more adept in this skill.

World of Dreams

The world of toys available through the 50s and early 60s was representative of my childhood in too many ways to describe. The choices for a youngster in the marketplace were often overwhelming, even for the more conventional classical toys. The popular fascination with science fiction through scary motion pictures about invariably evil extra-terrestrial aliens, the prolific glossy sci-fi magazines and the fantasy children's comics only fuelled this demand. It probably peaked with the dramatic introduction of the 'Space Age' in October 1957 with the successful launching of Earth's first artificial satellite. Now that rocket travel was a reality, consumer demand by children for anything heralding space travel, including rocket ships, flying saucers, robots and ray guns became frenetic.

To keep a sense of perspective about which toys were more important to children in that era, I have selected both popular as well as some uncommon objects to best describe this phenomenon. At the expensive 'high end' of this vast array were pedal cars. Every boy usually dreamed of owning one at some point in their young lives, but only a privileged few were that fortunate. The basic models such as the Nobby and the Moon cars were little more than a metal seat and steering wheel enclosed in a simple frame perched on four wheels.

These economy models ranged modestly in price from £1 to £3 in the early 50s. The more sophisticated Australian 'Cyclops' pedal cars, such as the ever popular Comet, the Thunderbird, or for older children, the Lightning, and the fancy imported English 'Tri-Ang' cars with ball-bearing crank drive, spoke wheels/rubber tyres, electric headlights and two-tone horn, usually retailed anywhere upwards of £8 to £16, and sometimes considerably more.[1]

The racy Cyclops Comet offered prospective owners a 'steel body with safety rolled edges. Crank drive, adjustable pedals, chrome plated hub caps.'[2] The Lightning car offered far more for children wishing to drive a pedal car:

> Chrome plated front bumper bar, headlights, parking lights, radiator grill and windshield. Large capacity boot with opening door, twin tail lights. Enamelled brilliant red. [3]

The brilliant red colour alone would have convinced me to part with my valuable cash which was a phenomenal cost for toys at the time. Put into perspective, the average male weekly wage in Australia in 1950/51 was only £22 and by 1960-61 was £43.[4] Consequently, it was fair to assume that the price of the more expensive pedal cars remained out of reach for most kids.

For many Australian children, it meant the homemade soapbox cart ('Billy cart') had to suffice to satisfy their enthusiasm for driving. For the Billy cart, all that was really needed was a sturdy set of four wheels affixed to a small wooden crate, a piece of rope to control the directional movement of the front wheels, and something comfortable on which to sit (brakes optional). Innovation was such a wonderful thing in the 50s.

Although not as costly but certainly high on a child's birthday or Christmas shopping wish list was the western-style cowboy outfit of a sombrero hat, suede suit comprising a vest and chaps, twin gun holster and most importantly, the cap-gun(s).These cowboy pistols were not just another gun, but a masterpiece of craftsmanship, beautifully fashioned to replicate vintage hand guns from the Old West, such as the Texan or the Colt. Our enjoyment of American cowboy favourites like Hopalong Cassidy ('Hoppy'), Roy Rogers ('King of the Cowboys') and the Lone Ranger (The masked former Texas Ranger) spawned other desirable cap-pistols eagerly sought by children.

Most die-cast revolvers fitted an entire roll of caps inside the cylindrical chamber, permitting repeated firing without the irritating need to regularly reload, as for single cap sidearms. In the early 50s, these six shooters were essential hardware for any aspiring cowboy or sheriff, and were modestly priced between ten and fifteen shillings each.[5] Besides, even if you had to wait for another Christmas or birthday before you eventually received the cowboy clothing, every cowboy still needed a cap-gun.

A subtle variation on this requirement to carry toy sidearms to fend off any likely foe was to own a space ray gun, capable of squirting a jet of water at high pressure out of a tiny hole at the muzzle, firing replaceable corks or producing a shower of harmless sparks. My preference was for the water pistol that was always particularly accurate, and the Atomic Water Pistol was ideal. Besides, it was guaranteed to atomise all space invaders. Conversely, the Australian-manufactured Atomic Power Pop-Gun only fired corks with a loud popping noise by using a brass plunger system, and came with a supply of four corks to ensure enough ammunition was always on hand.

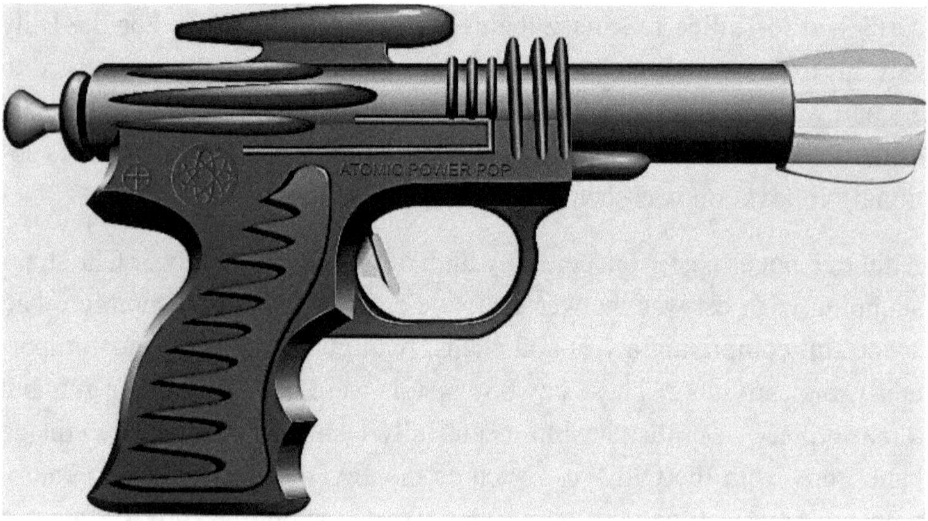

Figure 32: Atomic Power Pop-Gun (Glenn, 1951)

Basic pop-gun rifles with the cork attached to a string for rapid recovery were also useful, but only for close encounters with the foe. When confronted by evil adversaries it was important to always have the right protection, and a ray gun was mandatory.

Of course, if a child was only looking for a ray gun that 'shoots with a bang and a flash' and nothing more, then the iconic Buck Roger U-235 atomic pistol was the solution. It was characteristically produced in two metallic finishes for authenticity, and as the advertising on its packaging promoted, it was 'absolutely harmless' as a ray gun. Unfortunately, it was also expensive and so restricted to those youngsters with sufficient pocket money.

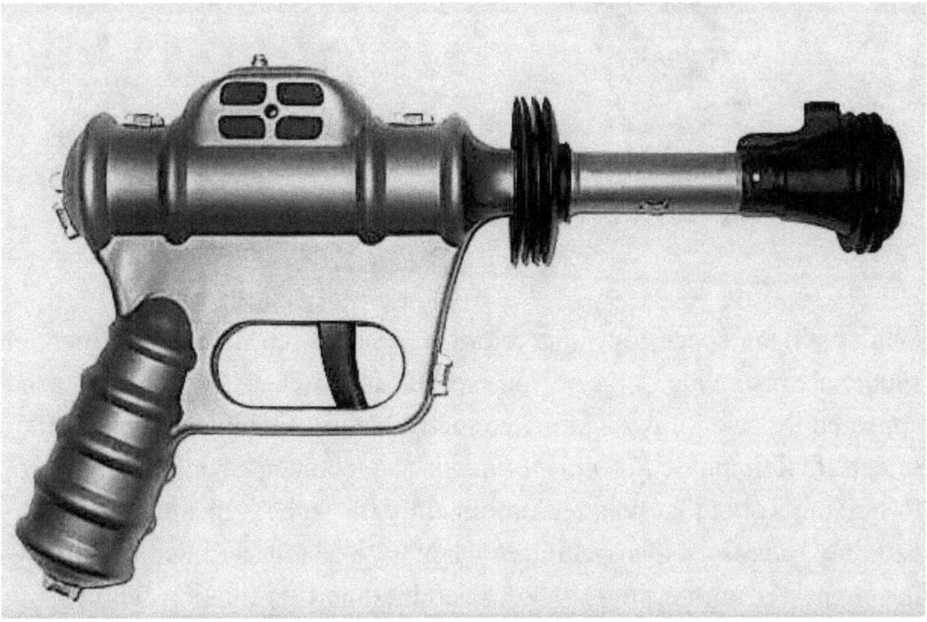

Figure 33: Buck Rogers U-235 Atomic Pistol (Daisy, 1945)

Then there was the Space Pilot Super-Sonic (Ray) Gun, complete with an elaborate high frequency regulator for ensuring three distinctive colours of green, red and white would flash from the muzzle, thereby eliminating any potential foe. An equally important decision that a youngster had to make.

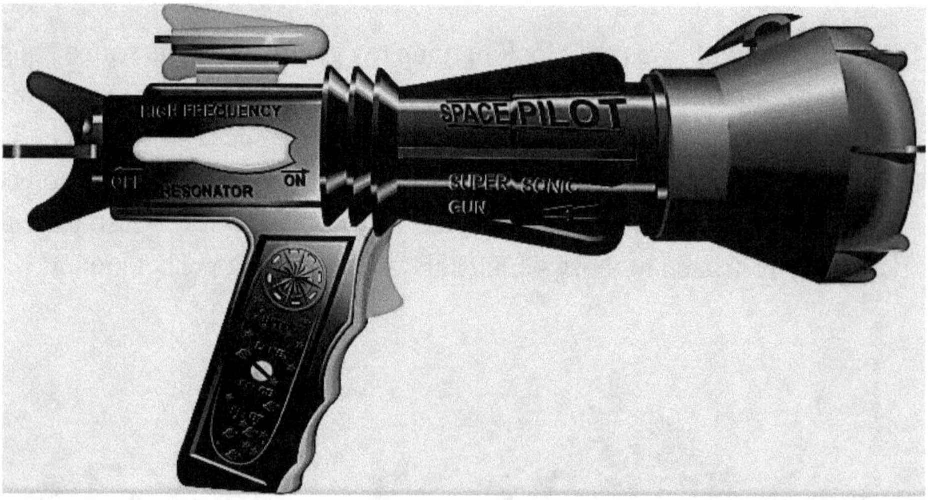

Figure 34: Space Pilot 3-Colour Super-Sonic Gun (Merit Toys, circa early 1950s)

Whilst still on space toys and futuristic devices, an honourable mention should also be made of the various spaceships, rockets and toy robots that appeared for sale following movies such as Metro-Goldwyn-Mayer's 1956 science fiction movie *Forbidden Planet*. The iconic mechanised automaton Robby the Robot that featured prominently throughout this motion picture certainly impressed many children when toy versions and that of other robots appeared in the mid-1950s.[6] The childhood fascination with robotic toys that had been around since the earlier part of the decade mainly displayed in books and comics suddenly flourished and boomed.

For the more classic toys, maritime vessels definitely deserve an honorary mention. One of my favourite Christmas presents of all time as a youngster had been a wooden hand-crafted model schooner that I described in a previous chapter, and regularly took to the beach. I had seen other models in toy shops but nothing as elaborate or as realistic as this expensive vessel. It sparked my nautical interests and soon I was interested in expanding my fleet with mechanically self-propelled boats. The most common variety were small clockwork ships and speed boats that required being wound-up and then released to power unaided across the water. The wind-up mechanism drove a flywheel-equipped propeller, with direction set manually via the stern-mounted friction rudder.[7] Off these little vessels would speed until encountering some unforeseen object that radically changed their course or caused them to unexpectedly sink. They were not expensive and created great mischief on the waterways. Besides, the next best alternative was an electric train set or a slot-car track, but the enormous price for these hobbies ensured that such toys always remained strictly a dream for me.

Given that television did not begin in Australia until late 1956, children readily provided their own entertainment, and toys were in abundant supply in the shops.

One particular perennial toy that had been around for centuries in various forms and yet continued to evolve was the rocking horse – a small horse mounted on wooden rockers similar to a rocking chair. In earlier decades, the lifelike horse included a mane and tail comprised of real hair and was fitted with a bridle, saddle and stirrups for a rider's comfort. For safety purposes, the horse might also be mounted on a fixed cradle of swing rockers for improved stability, minimum vibration and to prevent it from toppling if ridden too vigorously.[8]

This second type of rocking horse was hung on a rigid immobile frame by iron straps.. Depending upon size of the child, the largest horse still retailed for up to £6. With the advent of more advanced toys for children from the Space Age in the late 50s, technology probably made the rocking horse less desirable and sadly consigned it to history as these innovative futuristic toys entered the market into the 60s.

Two unusual toys that perhaps signify that transition period are Pick-Up Sticks and the Hula Hoop. Prior to television in Australia, I played Pick-Up Sticks (now also known as 'Fiddle Sticks') regularly as it involved considerable physical skill and patience to successfully complete. The game involved a bundle of 31 small wooden sticks, each eight inches (20 centimetres) long with five of each bright colour (pink, orange, yellow, green, blue and purple) painted at their ends, as well as one black stick.[9] Each colour group was assigned different points, with the solitary black painted stick having the highest points.

The bundle was dropped by hand into a jumbled loose bunch onto a table and all sticks of the same colour had to be removed in turn by a player with a stick or 'tool' one at a time from the overall pile without disturbing any other stick until the entire select group was collected. A player who disturbed a secondary stick lost their turn and the next player resumed the process by removing a group of a different colour. The winner was the player who amassed the highest score once all sticks had been removed from the bunch.[10]

This game of skill required a particularly steady hand and substantial enduring patience to be successful, unlike the following game that required a vastly different temperament. The modern Hula Hoop became remarkably popular with girls in Australia around 1958, despite the distractive introduction of television. It remained extremely popular well into the 60s and defied many pundits who predicted it was a passing fad.

It was a summertime recreational pursuit that was pursued with vigour as girls mastered the various techniques of twirling the plastic rings around their waist, neck or limbs (usually in one manoeuvre), as well as many other derivations (throwing and catching) with single or multi-coloured hoops. If that was not difficult enough when simply standing, try doing it whilst walking. The hoops were hollow, lightweight, flexible and importantly, they were affordable for youngsters. The phenomenon never completely disappeared although it declined considerably over the years until a new generation eventually embraced it again in the late 1990s.

The world of children's toys has always been a wonderful world of dreams and imagination for youngsters, and the golden era certainly provided me with ample scope to dream about such matters. In so many ways, it was a privileged time to enjoy such toys or at the very least, aspire to eventually own toys that provided great pleasure for youth.

The Right Way

There is a rather astute saying that every job should only be done once, and that is 'the right way' first time. There are many ways to do a job, depending upon who you are and what you are doing, but the fundamental principle still prevails – 'waste not, want not.'

The 50s period in Australia was not initially an era providing much technological assistance for domestic chores compared with today's resources, and in our home, manual labour seemed the most successful way to get most jobs done. Before most modern innovative domestic appliances were invented, 'elbow grease' prevailed, involving rolling up your shirt sleeves and getting the job done. Let me start with bugs in the air, usually around foodstuffs or generally a nuisance in the home. For ants, a little Borax sprinkled liberally around their nest did the trick. For flies, it was the draconian extermination technique known as 'ruthless swatting'.

For earwigs, the most unlikely insects to inhabit your residence, it was a recommended course of chemical eradication, namely paradichlorobenzene crystals (fumigant, insecticide and repellent) liberally sprinkled about a room to keep down their numbers. Now you had to be a proficient industrial chemist as well as a homemaker.

If I inadvertently swallowed one of these airborne beasties, my mother's remedy for me was always to lie down and rest to recuperate sufficiently. We were most fortunate to never incur any plagues of field mice because I am sure that it would have involved a dedicated 'slash and burn' approach with no survivors. Moths were an entirely different matter. There were only limited solutions available to eradicate them from eating their way through every item of clothing inside our house – kill the moth directly or "mothball" them with long term patience by using the reliable camphor (mainly naphthalene) balls as a suitable deterrent. To this day, I am still unsure why insects were treated so poorly.

A far less punitive measure was the moth preventer marketed as Petal Dust. The name itself was intriguing, supported by the following advertising description: 'Petal dust is a concentration of the loveliest sweet-scented flowers blended with the beautiful air-purifying properties of pines and rare trees.' I can only suppose the product lulled the moths into a false sense of security, as the advertising also added the ominous warning that 'PETAL DUST means death to all moths'.[1]

I am unclear why advertisers were so pre-occupied with nature in those days, but the following advertisement for artificial silk certainly got my attention:

> Lustrous coils of transmuted sunshine: Sunshine poured into the forest, through the long and by-gone years. Fed on sap the leaves and branches lived again in verdant green.
>
> Thro' the ages dreamed the forest; lovely, lonesome, unexplored. Then came Science with its magic: waved a wand and, lo – From the trees that once stood sturdy, 'gainst the tempest's cruel beat, came a wealth of lustrous fibres; shining, gleaming, dazzling, fair – Sylvan Artificial Silk.[2]

Native bees and their hives were an entirely different menace and a conundrum for my mother. When they nested in nearby trees the hive generated considered airborne traffic, and it was to be carefully avoided. Such an attractive natural reservoir of honey was always difficult to resist and it was only the foolhardy that risked retrieving any of this bounty. Anyone bitten by an angry bee quickly learned to avoid irritating them in the future.

Even large white witchetty grubs had their place in our natural environment at home, and from time to time, Dad used to uncover them whilst digging in the loamy soil and eat them for their immense protein content. This indigenous bush tucker was something that he learned about whilst working in the remoter northern regions of Australia in his younger years, and they did taste alright, albeit something of an acquired taste and not for me.

Our family nearly always mended or repaired household and property items rather than replace them. In the 50s, soldering became an everyday skill for my father. With a basic soldering iron, a tin of flux paste and a stick of tinman's solder, nothing was too difficult to fix. Enter the domestic metallurgist for problem solving on the home front. His self-taught proficiency with the soldering iron meant almost anything metal, precluding aluminium, could be fixed at short notice.

My mother's speciality was more associated with the home, and making preserves of fruit and vegetables. Jams were her speciality, particularly blackberry, plum and marmalade as well as trying her hand at pickles and sauces, such as mushroom and home-made mayonnaise. From time to time, we might also be provided with something far more exotic, such as dried local fruits.

The problem with growing your own plums in the home garden was the abundance of native birdlife that routinely feasted on this bounty, and consequently left much of the fruit disfigured or destroyed. Forget about mesh netting or perhaps drastic scare techniques to frighten the birds – the most environmentally friendly approach was to ensure they were well fed and thus not interested in all our delicious plum trees. One plum tree in the garden was sacrificially assigned for the birds, and the remainder excluded by carefully securing our pet goat in immediate proximity. Fortunately this Nanny-goat did not fancy plums but her presence around the other trees was certainly enough to discourage any bird feasts.

Personal cleanliness was another area where there was only one right way in our family, and beware those not prepared to conform. After enjoying a typical adventurous day exploring the bushland around the district, rolling down sand dunes and climbing gigantic trees, it was not unusual for me to arrive home covered from head to toe in dirt, dust and sometimes tree sap. I am probably understating the situation, as my appearance resembled more that of a bedraggled scarecrow than a young boy. The first priority was always to wash my hands and ideally scrub under the fingernails before presenting at the dinner table. If my scruffy appearance was beyond a simple hand wash, it was time for a hot bath and this was usually a very protracted process to organise enough scalding hot water for the job.

Two types of soap were always on hand – the ever-reliable and heavy duty pumice grit Solvol soap for the preliminary clean, and a softer Velvet soap for a smooth finish. Hair washing was optional but usually managed to get done amongst all the resultant suds. A clean face was mandatory and may have required slightly more diligence. Further scrubbing of feet and toenails may also have been warranted if my bush exploration antics had involved being barefoot at any stage. When all the body washing was completed, there was still the final inspection process to be endured, and this was always conducted by my mother to ensure a respectable youngster presented for a home-cooked meal.

Family values in those days traditionally focused on ensuring a child grew up without any serious health issues or potential deformities likely to impact on their later lives as adults. If young teeth were likely to develop crooked or protruding, wearing fitted wire braces became mandatory for several years to address the problem. If a child's eyesight was poor and spectacles were essential, even the cruel taunts of other children such as 'four-eyes' or 'goggle-eyes' still had to be endured. In those bygone days, children's spectacles usually had thick cumbersome frames or lightweight wire ones. The intent was upon providing quality lenses to improve eyesight rather than making a fashion statement with fancy frames, so we had to grin and bear it.

If a child walked with an awkward gait or routinely slouched when seated, the remedy was to constantly admonish them verbally until they learned to do walk or sit with the right posture (chin up, shoulders back and straight). In extreme cases, it meant wearing a back-brace girdle to ensure straightening of the developing spine. Interestingly, primary schools reinforced these measures through their routine daily processes for children – marching in regimented squads, sitting up straight in class, standing to attention at morning assembly and not answering back unless requested by the teacher. Discipline and order to instil a sense of purpose in each child was essential.

The impetus from parents was to raise children who were clean, neat and well-dressed, which represented to others an indication of your social respectability. Children were expected to behave reasonably in public, always respect their elders and never interrupt their parents at any time. They were to be seen but not heard. Manners and politeness were essential for a child of the 50s, with formal education viewed as the most important ingredient to developing them outside of home life. As a consequence, scholastic homework became obligatory and although play time was important, it was permitted only after homework was completed.

From a child's perspective, the freedom to play with other kids and to undertake an entire range of enjoyable pursuits without adult supervision was the Australian way. Of course, sometimes and probably more often than was acceptable, children could stray from the right way parents expected of them. The following abbreviated quote illuminates the antics that children indulged in if left too much to their own devices:

> Our feet were like leather and we knew little fear. Tricky climbs up vertical factory walls and over crumbling back fences to get a ball… wagging school, back-lane fights, rock fights…wandering miles never lost…The games we played were universal… gutter marbles, Queenie, cowboys-and-indians, hopscotch, piggyback races. We played until our Mums leaned over the front balcony and yelled our names up and down the street for tea.[3]

A child's mother always knew the right way to do anything and sometimes they were feared more than the father. In our family, my mother was responsible for all home matters from preparing meals, baking and cooking, dish washing, doing the laundry and ironing clothing, washing the children when needed, mending clothing, sending the children to school, cleaning the house interior and making new clothes for the children, to tackling outdoor projects like hand mowing grassy areas of the property, managing the brood of chickens, and catching snakes. She also looked after the garden and grew plum trees.

In the 1950s, it was universally expected that married women would be the home-maker and attend to most domestic chores requiring their skills.

If raising children, they were expected to provide most of the nurturing and guidance needed to teach their offspring the distinct differences between right and wrong. Upsetting the matriarch by use of foul language, deceit, dishonesty, theft or fighting was tantamount to a criminal offence by a child. A lesser offence would be not offering your seat on a train or tram to the disabled or infirmed, any women or the elderly. Social mores of those times demanded that children show respect and exhibit politeness whenever necessary, and refrain from hooligan behaviour.

My father's home responsibilities were directly linked to outdoor activities involving strenuous works, such as clearing vegetation, wood chopping, clearing roof gutters, repairs to the house and the twin bungalows, and of course, driving our car. They were as important and essential to developing a semi-rural property as the interior home duties. His role as a provider did not extend to working outside of our property.

When it came to childhood disciplinary punishment, the usual consequence came in the form of an immediate response from my mother, without any chance of a reprieve. This may range in diversity of penalties from going without an evening meal and an early bedtime, confinement to home on a weekend, additional or harsh chores, or loss of pocket money for a week, to the infamous mouth-washing process with soap. The solutions were virtually endless and effective.

If a child's naughty behaviour warranted serious punishment, my father was assigned the onerous task. Sometimes a reprieve would be granted, or a second chance offered. On other occasions, the matter would be deemed to be unpardonable and the inevitable sentence for the childish disobedience carried out.

This involved my father's shaving razor strop that was a long, flexible, two-sided strap of tough leather. Its primary use was to polish and burnish his straight blade razor. By gently drawing the blade edge or 'stropping' it *spine-first* along the leather in a series of careful strokes to avoid cutting into the leather, the blade's sharpness is increased markedly. The strop remains a traditional sharpening implement hung on the wall in barber shops even today, and in our home, it remained on a hook almost all the time.

Its secondary use was to administer suitable punishment which was relatively rare in our family yet incredibly effective. One or two slaps with the strop across buttocks known as 'getting strapped' was always sufficient to reinforce that unacceptable behaviour was not to be repeated. In hindsight, these harsh punitive measures did work. I certainly have no residual resentment about them, especially as my father only ever used the strop as a last resort after all other disciplinary solutions had been exhausted. In many ways, the childhood fear of being strapped was the best deterrent to any future atrocious behaviour.

It is interesting to reflect that such childhood punishment was commonplace in most domestic and school environments in Australia in the 1950s, albeit a rather severe measure of discipline. I suppose that as there was such public acceptance of corporal punishment in schools throughout Australia, it was not unreasonable to accept that parents could provide the same measures in the home. There was certainly no mass demonstrations amongst the populace about such matters to my recollection.

For whatever reason, there were always some individuals through my life who rarely managed important matters in the right way. One such person was a boy at my primary school who was usually the last child to be chosen on any sporting team. At lunch breaks when impromptu games like softball, soccer or Australian Rules football games might be convened, this boy was without exception the last to be chosen to play in the group. When he did get a game, it was inevitable that his side would lose. I recall that he had difficulty consistently catching a softball, perhaps marking a football, or for that matter staying on his feet. Whether he was naturally clumsy or merely uninterested, the end result was usually inevitable.

He was rarely selected for group athletic events such as team relays or tunnel ball, because he would be the one who dropped the relay baton or missed the ball and lost the race for his team. Surprisingly, he never quit despite relentless failures and was always keen to be selected again. If I learned anything about this unfortunate lad, it was his dogged persistence to succeed at any cost, in spite of his many mistakes and occasional injuries. He probably would have been better suited to less energetic pastimes, but in the 50s, most children thoroughly enjoyed participating in competitive sports.

Children's pocket money rarely stretched far enough at any time, given the incredible range of confectionery, soft drinks and toys readily available in the 50s, making it hard to learn how to save. Even our parents realised this economic dilemma. The solution was obvious and the remedy, or namely the right way, was diligently saving any spare coins in a moneybox provided by the local branch of my family's bank. My tin moneybox resembled the bank's city office building and could easily hold about £1 worth of coins. These cleverly designed money traps permitted any coins to slide inside but were then irretrievable without cutting open the entire container. Just to ensure the entire fiduciary process was traceable, the bank provided each child with a personal passbook to record the deposit. These always made me feel like a grown-up.

Saving money became an important learning tool for many young children and every couple of months when my full moneybox was deposited with the bank, the amount was added to my passbook. I recall eventually amassing somewhere approaching the staggering sum of £22 over a few short years, with compound interest. In today's terms, this represents a modern day equivalent value of $615 as at 2016.[4] Quite a tidy sum of money for a 12-year-old. Possessing a passbook with my name displayed and an ever-growing balance of money certainly taught me fiscal responsibility from an early age and how to manage frugally within my economic means. One other benefit of this process was my father would often purchase my sweets to compensate my meagre pocket money.

Perhaps one of the most important right ways for a child in the 50s was clearly knowing the difference between right and wrong. It always seemed easier and sometimes sociably acceptable to do anything the wrong way, but doing it the right way required individual effort and consideration for others. There were many wrong ways to distract a youngster, including smoking behind the school woodshed, wagging school, foul language, fighting, being untruthful, stealing and bullying, hurting other children, harming animals and damaging property. To display respect and courtesy took hardly any personal effort, and good manners were easy to follow.

Many children opted to do the wrong thing and reaped the consequences from their teachers. Sensible discipline was important for any child's early development because it established the ground rules for social behaviour in a community. It drew a demarcation line in the sand for everyone. Being a larrikin or prankster has always been an integral part of the Australian culture for children and adults alike, and I have no doubt, every school had many such characters. In fact, such mavericks are often highly esteemed amongst their peers because they appear unique and thus likeable. The right way for the majority of us has always been based upon the intangible assets of good manners and courtesy which are not always seen as rebellious enough by some youth.

Everything is Changing

The eventual introduction of television to our home at the beginning of 1961 was initially exciting to me but subsequently disappointing as transmissions were only in black and white, and our local reception quality was somewhat variable. Often the program being viewed would distort into shaky lines, the picture commence rolling up or down the screen or even cease to appear, followed by the TV station's test pattern and an apology regarding faulty transmission. At other times, scheduled programs were cancelled without warning or replaced with something totally uninteresting. The presence of the large TV set also dramatically segregated our evening family arrangements; from a cosy group who collectively listened to the radio after dining, to watching only specific television programs of interest, either individually or together.

> To accommodate TV, the lounge room changed seemingly overnight. Suddenly it had an informal atmosphere; lower, lighter furniture; subdued lighting; and a layout that shifted the focal point of the room from the open fireplace (at least in winter) to the TV set.[1]

As a young child, there really only was one local show on the TV worth watching, and it was '*The Tarax Show*' that screened every weekday between 5 pm and 6 pm. This pioneering program was extraordinary for a number of reasons. It was the first regular live children's show on GTV Channel Nine in Melbourne, premiering on 21st January 1957, only two days after the official opening of the television station. Launched as '*The Happy Show*', it ran continuously from 1957 until 1964. It featured a mix of variety, music, dance, educational segments, comedy, stories and drama for children from a resident cast of Channel Nine personalities.

The program eventually changed its name to *The Tarax Show* sometime around 1959 to reflect the sponsor; the Melbourne-based soft drink manufacturer Tarax Drinks Company.[2] To even have a sponsor was quite a feat as sponsors were scarce in the early days of Australian television.[3]

So much Tarax [soft drink] came to be sold through the popularity of this program, that they made increasing capital outlays to cope with the demand for their product.[4]

In its earliest days, *The Happy/Tarax Show* was hosted by the likeable and irrepressible Happy Hammond dressed in his colourful trademark chequered suit and hat. In 1960, it was "King Corky, King of the Kids" (Geoff Corke), complete with his regal cloak and crown, and later the show was hosted by Uncle Norman (Norman Swain). Always present as co-host was the cheeky and loveable Gerry Gee — together with ventriloquist Ron Blaskett. Such was Ron's skill as a ventriloquist that children quickly recognised that Gerry was the star personality in the show as he was cheeky, loveable, quick-thinking, smart, and most importantly, appealed both to the children and adult viewers alike.[5]

Gerry Gee was definitely unique in Australian television entertainment in the late 50s, and his presence always conjured something unusual and typically hilarious on the program. It made for compulsive childhood viewing each afternoon. During the era of King Corky, Gerry appeared as a court jester seated on a small throne beside the King's throne. Through the magic of television and some smart gimmickry, the ventriloquist's doll came to life and '…enabled Gerry to hold Tarax drinks, tickle Corky with a feather duster and generally add a new dimension to the character'.[6]

Ventriloquist Ron Blaskett seemingly recognised the immense scope for Gerry Gee as evidenced by more of his edited excerpts:

> …His humour had to be relevant to what kids thought and felt at that time … that adults would feel involved and favourably disposed towards the character...if he stepped out of line, I was the person to quickly show him the error of his ways. Any infraction, and it would be "off to the woodshed"…[7]

> ...as I started to work with him, although he seemed to weigh a ton on my arm, I realised the great expressions I could extract from him. One particularly good movement was the way his eyes could be rolled upward with a look of disgust. Not many figures have been made around the world with this ability. The fact that he could poke his tongue out was also an advantage — particularly for ice-cream commercials that came later.[8]

I was so impressed with Gerry Gee that I immediately became a member of the Gerry Gee Tarax Club on 14th February, 1961, barely a few weeks after our family owned a television set. As Member No. 89226, I also received an impressive small diamond-shaped brass badge, with an enamelled design of Gerry Gee's face on a blue background, along with my official authorised certificate and congratulatory letter.

Figure 35: Gerry Gee Tarax Club

However, I really wanted to see Gerry Gee in person, so on my 11th birthday in late 1961, my mother took me into the show at Channel Nine studios in Richmond. I was not disappointed. Along with a large group of other enthusiastic youngsters as an audience, we participated in the show, even going on television to receive a birthday gift. Gerry Gee was certainly realistic in person, and seemed to me as life-like as his physical appearance. It was a memorable experience.

Probably the only other local television show worth viewing was late in the evening; the famous '*In Melbourne Tonight*' (IMT) hosted by Graham Kennedy, Australian entertainer and variety performer extraordinaire. Graham's hilarious and unpredictable antics always made watching the show compulsory viewing because just about anything could happen. He was the master of delivering impromptu comedy, even turning innocuous moments such as product advertisements into something outrageous.

Advertisers would pay a fortune to have him send up their products on TV, believing that one Kennedy insult was worth 10 times the praise from a lesser performer. He gave them value for money, with the record for a Kennedy advertisement of 10 minutes.[9] Graham was also Frankston's favourite famous resident, living in a house perched on the top of a cliff on Oliver's Hill which was the highest topography overlooking Port Phillip Bay:

> ... I've just recently purchased a place in Frankston, where I was originally. I thought I wanted to be closer to the city, and I don't. I want all the water around me. It's about 40 minutes from Melbourne city. I travel off-peak which is beaut. And I have a driver. It's a nine-roomer and not as old as I'd like it to be. Its feature is the view. It's right on the top of the hill and all you've got in front of you is water.[10]

The introduction of black and white TV transmissions to our home suddenly provided a plethora of American serials to us, hitherto unknown or restricted to radio. Now we had visual representation of programs without having to go our nearest picture theatre in Frankston. The list of overseas programs was virtually endless, with an avalanche of westerns, drama serials and comedy shows readily available on your screen to suit every taste. My favourite westerns were the legendary *Bonanza*, *Rawhide* with a youthful Clint Eastwood as Rowdy Yates, *Rifleman* with grinning Chuck Connors, and of course *Have Gun Will Travel* with the tough and immovable

Richard Boone.

Comedies like *I Love Lucy, Candid Camera* and *Sergeant Bilko* were only surpassed by the suspenseful, action-packed nightly serials such as secret agent *Jet Jackson* or *Sea Hunt* with the aquatic Lloyd Bridges. Perhaps *Perry Mason* with the clever Raymond Burr and *77 Sunset Strip* about private investigators with the super cool sidekick 'Kookie' played by Edd Byrnes attracted more audiences. The sheer choice of programs was astounding at that time.

My transition from primary schooling with less than 100 pupils attending from our semi-rural local district to secondary schooling closer to Frankston with at least several hundred students was never going to be easy. The big fish in a small pond now became a very small fish in a gigantic ocean of other children. It was 1963 and the times were changing. The personal freedoms and uninhibited ways of the 50s and early 60s were disappearing as population growth in neighbouring Frankston exploded.

The first massive housing estate constructed nearest to our district was aptly named *Karingal* that was thought to be an Aboriginal (Koori) expression describing a good camp ('happy camp'). The name was initially adopted by the new high school built on the estate that opened in 1961 on the urban fringe between Frankston and nearby Langwarrin. Builders A.V. Jennings, who were the largest private building firm in Australia in those post-war years, opened their first display homes on this estate in 1962.[11] By 1963 when I started high school, Karingal still only offered Years 1-4, with the remaining Year 5 and Year 6 classes yet to commence.

I considered myself rather fortunate compared to my sister who was three years older and commenced her secondary schooling in 1960 in temporary 'classrooms' located in the Life Saving Club on the Frankston beach. I recall her informing me about occasional concerns when seawater sometimes reached the classroom on stormy days and students had to keep their feet dry until the unusual high tide retreated. This was strictly a short-term measure whilst the new high school was under construction on Ashleigh Avenue in Karingal.

The new grand housing estate of Karingal eventually took about 12 years to complete the 3000 homes, but the local high school was full to capacity by 1965, attracting students from all surrounding residential and rural areas. By the late 1980s, the high class development on rural land known as Karingal reached a staggering 4000 dwellings housing about 13,000 people.[12] This massive suburban development was only a relatively short distance from the boundary separating Frankston and Langwarrin.

Gone for me were the free-spirited days of long walks to and from primary school, complete with a myriad of adventures on each journey, to be replaced with the mundane weekday schedule of catching a school bus and wearing a distinctively labelled school uniform (shirt with a tie, jumper, blazer, trousers and black shoes and long socks). Suddenly my physical appearance was important as students were considered to be representatives of the school. There were dress standards to follow, including no untidy, unkempt or long hair over the shirt collar for boys.

Studying and daily homework became essential and mandatory duties, undertaking up to nine subjects per academic year. The learning regime relied upon considerable and often heavy text books. This meant incessantly carrying these text books between classes all day or home after school, reading text books and eventually storing many text books in a personal locker that was secured with a key carried by myself. A regime of structure and discipline became the norm. Attending classes with up to thirty others squeezed into the classroom and learning various subjects such as mathematics (algebra, trigonometry, geometry), geography, science, English expression, English literature, French, woodwork, physical education and social science became the new order of my education process.

An entire universe of new subjects was now compulsory learning. Perhaps most disconcerting, life had become highly competitive amongst fellow students in sporting prowess and academic achievements. I was barely even selected in some sports let alone successful in any others. Apart from my own sister who was three years older attending the same school, I knew nobody at all amongst the hundreds of students enrolled. It was the start of a new challenging period of my life and definitely the beginning of the end of my golden era.

This form of culture shock was sudden and permanent, particularly for someone residing in a semi-rural/rural environment. I was surrounded by virtual strangers, had to make new friends from scratch, and attended prolonged consecutive 40 minute classes that were strictly regimented and co-ordinated each day. There were personal storage security lockers for text books, unusual subjects like woodwork and the French language to study, hordes of students around all the time, mandatory homework each night, and a complete reliance upon a bus for transport between home and school, crowded with fellow students. If I missed that early morning or late afternoon bus, I had a very long walk indeed.

The first year of my secondary schooling in 1963 also introduced me to the traumatic aspect of childhood bullying. As I initially knew none of my new classmates for the first few weeks of school, it was relatively easy to be targeted by the local bullies looking for any vulnerable candidates that lacked a group of friends for support. As the saying goes; 'there is safety in numbers'. There were three bullies in this particular group of larrikins who were boisterous, disruptive in class and generally caused mischief most of the time. When they were not being sent before the headmaster for disciplinary attention, they were bullying other pupils or vandalising school property.

The title of drongo or numbskull seemed to be more appropriate terms to describe these characters, as they certainly had little interest in gaining a secondary education, and in turn devoted themselves to harassing or hurting other students. Fortunately for me, their poor attendance and academic records eventually backfired on them, and two of the group left school the following year. The remaining larrikin was left to flounder without his bully associates, and paradoxically found himself without any friends at all. It was a sad outcome for their education but a satisfying result for me.

Coincident to this new phase in my late childhood/early teenage years was the tenure of Mr George Douglas (universally known as 'Jud'), the founding principal of Frankston East (later Karingal) High School in Victoria. Mr Douglas was the school's longest serving headmaster (1959-1992)[13] and father of the famous intrepid adventurer, filmmaker and enthusiastic conservationist Malcolm Douglas who spent much of his life travelling throughout the Kimberley region of Western Australia on the opposite side of Australia to Victoria. I also spent many years of my adult life living in the same coastal area of the West Kimberley regularly frequented by Malcolm when he conducted many of his wildlife studies and travel documentaries. It can be a small world.

Life at home for me quickly became a welcome sanctuary to retreat from the numerous demands of secondary education, It provided a place of stability and familiarity in times when my entire world seemed to be changing radically, but such is the nature of change, and without change, we cease learning.

End of my Golden Era

I am unsure when the golden era of my own childhood precisely finished as it was probably over a series of unforeseen or even unrelated events, starting with my secondary school education and coinciding with my early teenage years. Personal interests changed, girls became more important in my daily life and educational routines became the norm rather than the exception. I lost contact with every one of my primary school friends within months, as none attended the same secondary school. My father passed on when I was 14 years of age which did not help this transition in the slightest.

At such a delicate age when entering those early teenage years, a boy's life can become complex and confusing. My father had always been extremely kind and generous towards me, particularly with respect to special rewards including confectionery. Perhaps as I was the youngest child in the family or we simply bonded well, he seemed to spoil me from time to time, despite my mother's emphatic objections. He was always attentive towards me even when busy on other tasks, if I was hurt when playing games, or needed some assistance completing my chores.

His death was totally unexpected with no prior signs of ill health and occurred during my term exam period at secondary school. Suddenly, my father was gone and only my mother remained to raise the three of us. He had worked incessantly to provide for us with limited financial resources and now, it was up to those left behind. I did not attend his funeral and instead went to school that sad day to avoid reliving the pain of his unexpected passing.

I believe unequivocally that the early teenage years are the most difficult as a boy sprouts into a young man, and leaves behind so many of those childhood interests. Then there is the terrifying facet of mixing with other young teenagers known as group 'peer pressure' and 'becoming accepted' in your social groups. Childhood is so brief, and perhaps the transition into teenage years is so subtle as to virtually pass unnoticed. Part of the answer may have been in my changing maturity as earlier adventures, pastimes and hobbies became less important to me. I had probably outgrown them when compared with my many new passions.

On the 14th February 1966, Australia introduced decimal currency for its notes and coins, replacing the British-style currency of pounds, shillings and pence. At the tender age of 15-years-old, I now had to deal with dollars and cents instead of my beloved shillings and pence. Gone was the ubiquitous large one penny coin and its half-brother, the smaller halfpenny, so fundamental when purchasing confectionery. They were replaced by the miniscule one cent piece (equivalent to a penny) slightly larger than a match head, and the modestly larger two cent (equivalent to two pennies) coinage. These coins were impossible not to lose, and if inadvertently dropped on the ground, literally became invisible to the naked eye. Try dropping a penny and its sheer size demanded your attention instantly. I rarely ever misplaced that coin.

Even more confusing, the beloved silver threepence and sixpence coins were no more, and a five cent substitute coin introduced for the latter. Most disturbingly, the magic one shilling piece that was so prized by youngsters as it represented twelve pennies, two sixpences or four threepences in value, was now a meagre ten cent coin. It all seemed unfair to me and a devaluation of our currency of sorts. Gradually, sweets were not able to be purchased by the pennyweight, and the five cent coin became the minimum measure for purchasing confectionery.

The man responsible for the creation of decimal currency coins was Stuart Devlin, a designer born in Geelong, near Melbourne in Victoria, who later became the Queen's official jeweller[7]. To his credit, the clever selection of Australian native fauna on these coins at least offset some of my dissatisfaction. His favourite was the platypus, depicted on the twenty cent coin that he considered his masterpiece.

Worse was still to come as sophisticated packaging of sweets appeared everywhere, and it became rare to be able to purchase unpackaged confectionery. Fancy foil wrapping in bright colours became the norm, so for example I had to purchase each delicious chocolate Freddo Frog individually rather than loose by the handful. Gone were the fascinating sealed glass jars brimming with individual delectable sweets strategically placed along counter tops to attract a youngster's attention, to be replaced with individually wrapped sweets encased in mundane, unimaginative and expensive cardboard packets or sealed in airtight plastic bags.

Bottled soft drinks now had a major competitor as metal cans assumed the mantle of convenience and popularity. Steel cans eventually surrendered to aluminium cans, and neither had any recyclable monetary value initially. Collecting and returning disused soft bottles for cash refunds no longer became a viable source of pocket money for me as the disposable society embraced soft drinks in cans which eventually became litter. It would only be years later that recycling the cans for their metal content would address the litter problem, but the halcyon days of cash refunds for soft drink bottles were definitely over.

Perhaps the demise of this era really started when people expected more and demanded change to suit. When anyone went to a petrol station in the 50s and early 60s, it was not simply to fill the fuel tank. It was to have the courteous attendant check the vehicle's engine oil level, radiator water level and occasionally replenish air in the car's tyres. The windscreen may have been cleaned as well, but most of all, it was a friendly experience chatting with the attendant and even possibly purchasing some snacks.

The modern era has deleted many such services in lieu of self-service, whilst still providing 'convenience foods'. It has appealed to the time-poor who have little or no interest in spending unnecessary time dealing with trivial matters such as routine vehicle maintenance checks. As automobiles became more electronic and less reliant upon a crank handle to start, so the reliable technology reduced the need for routine vehicle checks.

The eventual passing of the golden era can only be partially attributable to technological advances, and most likely also resulted from a shift in people's attitudes. In the 1950s, the Friday night ballroom dances, gala balls, fancy dress nights, and so many other celebratory functions were usually convened in the one place – the Langwarrin district hall, and virtually everyone came along. Fetes and fairs were held at the local primary school or churches, and were always well attended. It was common to see locals from anywhere in the district at community sporting events, both as participants and spectators.

However, as the farmlets and larger tracts of unoccupied land were sold and subdivided for housing, so the local population increased enormously, and householder interests probably became more focused on local issues rather than district issues. With this urbanisation and the flood of residential housing on increasingly smaller land allotments, the original local community spirit so prevalent in Langwarrin in those earliy days of my childhood changed to that of a suburban society. People no longer knew who lived in their street or in their local area, and with that disinterest came the disintegration of earlier close-knit community-related groups.

Our family resided in the district for almost 50 years until both my parents eventually passed away and as adult siblings, we pursued our lives and endeavours elsewhere in Australia. We were so fortunate to have been raised in this district during such a pioneering period, regardless of the various hardships and struggles of starting such a new life. The benefits of an upbringing in this era of personal freedoms and overall community spirit certainly outweighed any difficulties experienced in that life. Most importantly to me was learning the invaluable life-long skills of having 'to go without' certain luxuries or even rudimentary necessities, as well as having 'to make do' with what I did possess. It certainly taught me the true value of worth, frugality and resourcefulness.

This knowledge has remained with me ever since. It is said that an experience gained is an experience shared. My memories of that era are all fond memories that greatly assisted me in later life and continue to endure today. I certainly miss those times, but as with everything great, all things come to an end.

In adult life, I was still able to savour various experiences produced during my childhood by eventual advances in technology. I call them reflections of the past. Many high quality motion pictures that were produced overseas from the period were either rarely exhibited in Australia, or I had been unable to view them due to my youth. Plenty more subsequently did not manage to be screened on television and remained in obscurity, probably stored away in cinematic archives for years. However, the advent of the digital optical disc (DVD) in 1995 was to change everything, with the capability to resurrect and convert original motion pictures into a portable digital storage format able to be purchased worldwide at a reasonable price.

Suddenly a raft of hitherto forgotten or mislaid movies resurfaced and were given a second lease of life. This eventually turned into a flood of resurgent nostalgia as so many of the old film classics became popular again. In some cases, motion pictures not considered as worthy for DVD processing remain elusive, but these are becoming fewer as the viewing public seeks more of these vintage films. The golden era encompassed British cinema in particular and the wealth of quality actors who starred in films throughout that period. These included those originating from a theatrical background on the British stage, perhaps even studying at the Royal Academy of Dramatic Art. Such performers often had a solid grounding in performing Shakespearean plays.

Sir Alec Guinness was just such an accomplished performer, whose impressive movie credits through the 1950s and early 1960s encompassed the gambit of comedy and drama. Some of his most humorous films included *The Lavender Hill Mob* (1951), *The Captain's Paradise* (1953), *The Lady Killers* (1955) and *Barnacle Bill* (1957), whilst his exceptional drama films include *The Bridge on the River Kwai* (1957), *Tunes of Glory* (1960) and *Lawrence of Arabia* (1962). Peter O'Toole, British-Irish actor who also starred in Lawrence of Arabia was in the equally dramatic film *Lord Jim* (1965). Sir Michael Redgrave was another outstanding actor who starred in classics such as *The Importance of Being Earnest* (1952) and *The Dam Busters* (1955).

I understand that the following quotation was provided by Sir Alec Guinness which captures those times so unpretentiously: 'I don't know what else I could do but pretend to be an actor.'

When it came to comedy, British actors ruled supreme, such as the irrepressible Peter Sellers in *The Mouse that Roared* (1959), *Lolita* (1962), and *Dr. Strangelove* or: *How I Learned to Stop Worrying and Love the Bomb* (1964)], the dour Alistair Sim in *The Belles of St. Trinian's* (1954) and *School for Scoundrels* (1960)], and the cheeky larrikin Sid James.

The list of dramatic actors was almost endless, and I briefly share only a few sentimental favourites of those delightful bygone days; David Niven [*Around the World in Eighty Days* (1956) and *55 Days in Peking* (1963)], Robert Newman [*Treasure Island* (1950)] Jack Hawkins [*The Cruel Sea* (1953)] and Australian legend Errol Flynn [*The Sun Also Rises* (1957)].

British television was also valued in the 1960s, with vintage comedians and comedy shows such as Tony Hancock, Eric Sykes, Ronnie Barker, Steptoe and Son, and Till Death Us Do Part with the indomitable character of Alf Garnett. Famous Hollywood actresses of that era also certainly deserve their due credit, such as Audrey Hepburn, Grace Kelly, Elizabeth Taylor, Katherine Hepburn and Natalie Wood.

American motion pictures became a dominant mainstay of Australia's viewing and an impressive number of classic quality feature films from the 1950s were ultimately released on DVD, such as *Sunset Boulevard* (1950), *The African Queen* (1951), *Shane* (1953), *From Here to Eternity* (1953), *On the Waterfront* (1954), *Forbidden Planet* (1956) and *North by Northwest* (1959). As a consequence, it was possible to regain a distinctive sense of the past by playing these vintage movies from your DVD collection. They were simpler, uncomplicated times in which these movies depicted that a story did not have to involve spectacular special effects, a convoluted script or a plethora of well-known actors, unlike today.

So many changes have happened to the wonderful things that I always took for granted in my childhood. The basic necessities of life, such as bread (now sliced and packaged), milk produced in cardboard cartons and not bottles that were refilled and often delivered to your home, fewer print newspapers, magazines and books replaced by electronic media without hardcopy, handwritten letters replaced by electronic email, and the introduction of alternative energy sources (solar, wind and geothermal) for domestic power consumption.

Mobile (cellular) telephones often linked to satellite coverage and a worldwide reliance upon computerised technologies were no longer in the realm of science fiction but now scientific fact. Aeroplanes and trains capable of supersonic or immense speeds, driverless vehicles, and space travel to the moon, to neighbouring planets and well outside of our solar system developed over the past 50 years. The increasing urbanisation of many developed countries, resulting in less and less rural space and more high density living within cities has been disconcerting. Dwelling space has now become an expensive commodity and high rise accommodation blocks proliferate.

I hope that city children still enjoy the freedoms and often unfettered choices that were afforded to me living in the wide open spaces, where having fun was not by playing on a computerised device nor organised by spending money, but arose from children simply being children playing outdoors. Such alternatives do not require technology, can be most satisfying and may even encourage you to seek better ways to enjoy yourself.

In the modern era, my childhood district of Langwarrin now appears to be an integral seamless part of endless suburbia with all the necessary elements of an urban area. Long gone are the extensive tracts of native bushland (excluding proclaimed reserves) and the innumerable orchards and poultry farmlets so prevalent in the 50s and early 60s. Bitumen roads, concrete footpaths, manicured parks, shopping centres, schools and more people are now the norm. Modern communications such as the Internet, television, mobile telephones and ubiquitous hand-held devices make the local community appear so much less important than in the past. News is now transmitted globally as it occurs.

I suppose that most metropolitan districts eventually undergo a transition from rural to urban, and for Langwarrin, this period has well and truly passed. However, I still feel privileged today to have experienced those pioneering days of the golden era, and in hindsight, it certainly benefitted my upbringing. As you travel on your journey through life, there are always distractions, deviations and delays before reaching the intended destination. Just remember that it is the travelling that is so very important and not the destination after all. So maybe bring your marbles and lollies in case there is yet another stopover on the journey.

Modern Childhood

Did my upbringing eventually improve the subsequent lives of my own children, and what qualities learned in my childhood did I believe could best contribute to their personal development? Both children were born in the early to mid-1970s into an era of flourishing technological change and the progressive introduction of computers and vastly improving electronic communications. Such technologies yielded an enormous range of advanced domestic appliances and sophisticated toys unknown in my golden era. By comparison with the 50s and 60s, my children were spoiled for choice.

Notwithstanding, the childhood learnings and values that I retained as an adult greatly assisted in their stable upbringing. Some human values are universal. Honesty, integrity, reward for effort through persistence and diligence, and a strong belief in oneself to succeed in endeavours rated highest from my earliest childhood. The ability to enjoy your life by not taking everything too seriously while treating others with due respect and courtesy also rank highly, as politeness towards others has never been a human weakness. Lastly, the enduring value of attaining the highest level of formal education for personal development should never be underestimated. I think that everyone should make the most of their lives and savour the journey.

Frugality is only learnt if the parent is prepared to teach the child and set the right example. My two children were raised from an early age for 10 years between the late 1970s and 1980s in a remote mining community on a substantial island off the Australian coast. As a consequence, they learned to cope and where necessary, to improvise with their limited resources. Their relative isolation from the mainland population provided many unique and enriching life experiences for them. Small communities provide great opportunities for children to thrive and to share in developing close friendships, much like in my early childhood. They made considerable friends on the island who still remain in contact as adults.

Their upbringing had a remarkably similarity to my own semi-rural life. They enjoyed considerable personal freedoms on a largely unpopulated island that fluctuated between 350-900 people over our 10 year tenure, until secondary education beckoned and relocation became necessary to reside in the nearest capital city. By the late 1980s, Australia provided considerably more opportunity for youngsters than ever before.

If there were any distinctive differences in raising the children compared to my early childhood, it was ensuring that they never went without any crucial necessities of life. To give your children the best opportunities to develop socially and educationally, you had to support, guide and nurture them along the way. If a child grows to be a well-mannered, trustworthy and decent person with a reasonable sense of humour and a preparedness to succeed in their working life, a parent could not wish for anymore.

Instilling such personal values before a child reaches adulthood is a long and tedious process, fraught with unnecessary distractions and short-cuts along the way. Life can present many difficult challenges and it is only by learning from these challenges that one develops as an adult. Manners may maketh the man, but life is based upon working to fulfil your dreams. I was particularly fortunate to have been raised by a struggling family in such an unprecedented era of domestic economic growth and development of our nation, and to have shared these positive childhood experiences with my own children. If it has assisted them along life's journey, then it was worthwhile because it certainly provided me with a great upbringing.

References

CHAPTER 1: The Changing Face of Australia

1. Lees and Senyard, *The 1950s: How Australia Became a Modern Society, and Everyone Got a House and a Car*, 1987, p.5.
2. Thomas, *The 1950s: Building a new Australia from the aftermath of war*, 2011.
3. Lees and Senyard, op.cit.,Synopsis.
4. Thomas, op. cit., pp.30-7.
5. Ibid., pp. 19-38, p.46.
6. O'Hanlon, *Home Together, Home Apart: Boarding House, Hostel and Flat Life in Melbourne*, c.1900-1940, 1999, p.11.
7. Brett, *Robert Menzies' Forgotten People*, 2007, p.23.
8. Pascoe, C., *Spaces Imagined, Places Remembered: Childhood in 1950s Australia*, 2011, pp. 59-72.
9. Howard, 'Marble Games of Australian Children', in *Child's Play: Dorothy Howard and the Folklore of Australian Children*, 2005, p.142.

CHAPTER 2: My Childhood Stamping Ground

1. Jones, *Frankston: Resort to City*, 1989, p.19, p.37.
2. Raworth and Turnor, *Frankston Central Business District Heritage Review*, 2010, p.6.
3. Jones, op.cit., pp.24-5.
4. Shaw, 'Permanent Settlement', in *A history of the Port Phillip District : Victoria before separation*,1996, p.58.
5. Jones, op. cit., p.50, p.63.
6. Arnall & Jackson, 'Brunswick', Victorian Municipal Directory, 1992. pp. 377–8, 695. Accessed at State Library of Victoria, La Trobe Reading Room.

7. Australian Bureau of Statistics, 'Total Frankston (SA2)', in 3218.0 – *Regional Population Growth, Australia*, 2014–15, 30 March 2016, ABS Canberra. Retrieved 29 September 2016.
8. Australian Bureau of Statistics, 'Langwarrin (State Suburb) Statistical Area Level 2 (SA2)', in *Regional Population Growth Data Summary for 2015*, 31 March 2017, ABS Canberra. Retrieved 16 May 2017.
9. Blake, *Place Names of Victoria*, 1977.
10. Scott, *The early history of Langwarrin*, 1966.
11. Ibid.
12. Morrison, 'Early History', in *Langwarrin settlers and soldiers*, 2008, p.147.
13. Ibid., 'Military Reserve', p.140.
14. Parks Victoria, 'Langwarrin Flora and Fauna Reserve – Park Notes', Department of Environment and Primary Industries, Government of Victoria. Retrieved 26 June 2017.
15. Ibid., 'Memories of Dorothy Capon nee Oates', p.104.
16. Ibid., 'Centreville', pp.154-5.
17. Wikipedia, 'Langwarrin', https;//en.wikipedia.orr/wiki/Langwarrin_Victoria, April 2017. Retrieved 16 May 2017.
18. Commonwealth Bureau of Census and Statistics, 'Langwarrin', in 2108.0, Volume II, Victoria, Part V Population and Occupied Dwellings in Localities with a Population of 50 persons or More, 30th June 1954, p.19.
19. Commonwealth Bureau of Census and Statistics, 'Langwarrin and Frankston', in 2107.0, Volume II – Victoria, Part V Population and Dwellings in Localities, 30th June 1961, p.18, p.24.
20. Wikipedia, 'Frankston', https;//en.wikipedia.orr/wiki/Frankston_Victoria, *When Hollywood Came to Melbourne: the story of the making of Stanley Kramer's On the beach* (17 December 2009), Australian Centre for the Moving Image, Retrieved 12 September 2015.

CHAPTER 3: Settling in Langwarrin

1. Wikipedia, 'Coolgardie safe', https;//en.wikipedia.org, Retrieved 9 February 2017.
2. Morrisson, op.cit., p.105.

3. Lees and Senyard, op.cit., p.56.
4. Wikipedia, 'List of number-one singles in Australia during the 1950s', in *David Kent's Australian Chart Book 1940-1969*, published 2005, https//en.wikipedia.org/wiki/ Kent_Music_Report. Retrieved 10 June, 2017.
5. Williams, 'September' in *Born in 1956? What else happened*? 2015, p.105.
6. Bedwell, *Suburban Icons - A Celebration of the Everyday*, 1992, pp. 16-17. Wikipedia, *Hills Hoist*, http://en.wikipedia.org. Retrieved 9 May 2017.
7. Murray, *A Home of My Own: Handy hints and images from domestic life in Australia in the 1940s and 1950s*, Mallon Publishing, Melbourne, 2001, p.27.

CHAPTER 4: Wildfires and Bonfires

1. Townsend, *Baby Boomers: Growing up in Australia in the 1940s, 50s and 60s*, 1988, p.86.
2. Davey and Seal, *A Guide to Australian Folklore: From Ned Kelly to Aeroplane Jelly*, 2003, p.78, p.148.

CHAPTER 5: The Domestic Life

1. Seddon, G., 'The Australian Back Yard', in *Australian Popular Culture*, edited by Ian Craven, 1994, p.22.
2. Williams, 'Food and Drink', in *Born in 1955? What else happened?*, 2015, pp.47-8.
3. Ibid., 'Food in Packets', p.39.
4. Murray, op.cit., p.66.
5. Reserve Bank of Australia, 'PreDecimal Inflation Calculator', http://www.rba.gov.au/ calculator/annualPreDecimal. Retrieved 16 August 2017.
6. Townsend, op.cit., p.54.
7. Bedwell, op.cit., p.84-5.
8. Reserve Bank of Australia, op.cit., Retrieved 16 August 2017.
9. Morrison, op.cit., p.151-2.

CHAPTER 6: Child's Play and Festivities

1. Leach and Fried (eds.), *Funk & Wagnalls Standard Dictionary of Folklore*, Mythology and Legend, one volume edition, 1972, p.153.
2. Howard, 'Counting-Out Customs of Australian Children', op.cit., p.133.

CHAPTER 7: Good Friends and Neighbours

1. Rowe, 'A Day Trip to the City by Ron', Chapter in *Hastings Memories: a collection of reminiscences*, 2007.
2. Australian Railway Historical Society (Victorian Division), 'Works' in *Newsrail* Monthly Magazine, Edition Issue March 1988, p.93.
3. Wikipedia, *Myrmecia (ant)*, https://en.wikipedia.org. Retrieved 21 April 2017.
4. Frankston City Council, 'Frankston's Geological Story and Map', in *Natural Reserves within Frankston City*, www.frankston.vic.gov.au, 2nd Edition, January, 2010, pp. 8-9.
5. Bowen, 'Sand Deposits', in *Geology of the Melbourne District*, Victoria, Geological Survey of Victoria, Bulletin No 59, 1967, pp.66-7.

CHAPTER 8: Primary School Early Days

1. Parkin, *Langwarrin, 100 years of Schooling 1890 – 1990*, p.4.
2. Morrison, 'Langwarrin Primary School', op.cit., p.184.
3. Arnold, H., 'Langwarrin', in *Place names and their meanings from the Casey Cardinia Region*, Casey Cardinia Libraries, http://www.cclc.vic.gov.au/placenames. Retrieved 15 May 2017.
4. Kent, J., *In the Half Light: Life as a Child in Australia 1900 -1970*, Angus and Robertson, North Ryde, New South Wales, 1988, p.211.
5. Morrison, 'Adderly Family', pp.7-9.
6. Pascoe, op.cit., p.171.
7. Watkins, 'Moorlands' 1948-1955', in *Readin' 'ritin' 'rithmetic: Stories of School and School Days from 1898-1986 from the Coomandook and Coonalpyn Areas*, 1986, p.69.

CHAPTER 9: The Senior Years

1. Archival Sauces, 'Making school children drink milk', 11 April 2011

https:// archivalsauces.wordpress.com.
2. Williams, 'Square-Dancing Craze', in *Born in 1950? What else happened?* 2016, pp.133-4.
3. Morrison, op.cit.,'Langwarrin Primary School', p.184.
4. Ibid., pp.184-5.

CHAPTER 10: The Corner Tuck Shop and Friends

1. Morrison, op.cit.,'Hutton Family', p.69.

CHAPTER 12: Fetes, Halls and Parties

1. Davey and Seal, op.cit.,'Meat Pies', p.187.
2. Morrison, op.cit., 'Langwarrin Football Club', p.177.
3. Davey and Seal, op.cit.,'Birthdays', p.38.

.

CHAPTER 13: Saturday Sport and Quiet Sundays

1. Morrison, op.cit., 'Tin Shed in Lloyd Park', p.150.
2. Wikipedia, 'Leigh Mathews', https// en.wikipedia.org. Retrieved 19 April 2017.
3. Morrison, op.cit.,'Cavill Family', p.41.
4. Townsend, op. cit., p.9, pp.72-6.
5. Ibid., 'The Clothes We Wore', p.45.
6. Wikipedia, 'Duffel coat', https://en.wikipedia.org. Retrieved 15 May 2017.

CHAPTER 14: Going to Town

1.Jones, op.cit., 'Introduction', p.19.
2.Williams, 'Food and Drink', in *Born in 1955? What else happened?* 2015, pp.45-6.
3. Lees and Senyard, op.cit., p.132.

CHAPTER 15: Beaches Near and Far

1. Bowler, 'Coastal Geomorphology – Beaches', *Port Phillip Survey 1957-1963. The Geology and Geomorphology, Memoirs of the National Museum of Victoria, No.27*, November 1966, p.28.
2. Short, *Beaches of the Victorian Coast & Port Phillip Bay: A Guide to*

Their Nature, Characteristics, Surf and Safety, 1966, p.177.

CHAPTER 16: Mornington Peninsula and More

1. Butler & Associates, 'Urbanising the Peninsula in the post-war era', in Mornington Peninsula Shire Thematic History, Attachment 5, July 2013, p.113.
2. Ibid., p.43.
3. Bratton, John, *The Teddy Bears Picnic*: Characteristic Two Step, M.Whitman & Son, New York, 1907, with lyrics by Kennedy, J., 1932.
4. Reserve Bank of Australia, 'PreDecimal Inflation Calculator', op.cit., Retrieved 16 August 2017.

CHAPTER 17: Collectibles and Other Interests

1.White, '"Americanization" and Popular Culture in Australia', in *Teaching History*, Vol 12, Part 2, August 1978, p.19.
2. Lees and Senyard, op.cit., p.133.
3. Commonwealth Bureau of Census and Statistics, 'Ages of the Population Urban and Rural Divisions', in 2108.0, Volume VIII, Australia, Part L Cross-Classifications of the Characteristics of the Population, Table 8, 30th June 1954, pp. 14.
4. Calabretta, M. and Ridge, C., *Tuckfields Birds and other cards: types, variants, chronology, exchange tokens, albums and miscellany*, Edition 3.0, www.calabretta.id.au., 2013, pp.1-5.
5. Bedwell, op.cit., p.73.

CHAPTER 18: The World of Dreams

1. Arnold, *Old Toys: identification and valuation guide*, 2004, p.6, p.16 & p.61.
2. Ibid., p.5.
3. Ibid., p.60.
4. Reserve Bank of Australia, '*4.17 Wages and Earnings*', https://www.rba.gov.au/statistics. Retrieved 28 June 2017.
5. Arnold, op.cit., p.16.
6. Bunte et al, *Vintage Toys: Robots and Space Toys*, 1999, pp.56-7.

7. Ibid., p.77.
8. Arnold, op.cit., p.34.
9. Museums Victoria, 'Game –Pick-Up Sticks', https//collections. museumsvictoria.com.au/ items/254275, Retrieved 28 June 2017.
10. Wikipedia, 'Pick-up sticks', https// en.wikipedia.org. Retrieved 28 June 2017.

CHAPTER 19: The Right Way

1. Braithwaite and Walsh, *Things My Mother Should Have Told Me*, 1991, p.159.
2. Ibid., p.30.
3. Bedson, Jack, in *The Endless Playground: celebrating Australian childhood*, compiled and edited by Paul Cliff, 2000, pp. 170-71.
4. Reserve Bank of Australia, 'PreDecimal Inflation Calculator', op.cit. Retrieved 16 August 2017.

CHAPTER 20: Everything is Changing

1. Groves, Derham, "There's more to 'televiewing' than meets the eye", in *1956: Melbourne, Modernity and the XVI Olympiad*, Museum of Modern Art at Heide, 1996, pp. 69-79.
2. Howson, Denzil, 'Tarax Show Memories', in The Tarax Show 1957-1964, Denzil Howson Archive, http://tdgq.com.au/tarax-show. Retrieved 12 June 2017.
3. Dick, Nigel, *The Tarax Show 1957-1964, Denzil Howson Archive.*
4. Blaskett, Ron, *You, Me and Gerry Gee: 60 Years of Australian Showbiz*, 2001, edited excerpts.
5.Howson, op.cit., 'January 1957 – Launch of The Happy Show'.
6. Blaskett, op.cit., 'The King Corky Era'.
7. Ibid., 'The Responsibilities of Gerry Gee'.
8. Ibid., 'The Creation of Gerry Gee'.
9. Cockington, J., *Mondo Weirdo: Australia in the Sixties,* 1992, p.169.
10. Ibid., p.168.
11. Monash University and The University of Queensland Joint Initiative, 'Karingal', in *Victorian Places*, www.

victorianplaces.com.au. Retrieved 17 June 2017.
12. Jones, op.cit., p.276.
13. Douglas, Flora, 'Surviving when things get tough', in *Frankston Standard Leader*, https://issuu.com/leadernewspapers/docs/frankston-leader, Issue 9 March 2009, p.8.

Bibliography

Arnold, Ken, *Old Toys: identification and valuation guide*, Crown Castleton Publishers, Bendigo, Victoria, 2004.

Australian Bureau of Statistics, *3218.0 – Regional Population Growth, Australia, 2014–15*, Australian Government Printer, ABS Canberra, 30 March 2016.

Australian Bureau of Statistics, Regional *Population Growth Data Summary for 2015*, Australian Government Printer, ABS Canberra, 31 March 2017.

Bedwell, Steve, *Suburban Icons - A Celebration of the Everyday*, ABC Enterprises, Sydney, 1992.

Blake, Les, *Place Names of Victoria*, 1st Edition, Rigby, Adelaide, 1977.

Blaskett, Ron, *You, Me and Gerry Gee: 60 Years of Australian Showbiz*, with Foreword by Bert Newton, Self -Published G Barrett and Associates, Doncaster East, Victoria, 2001.

Brett, Judith, *Robert Menzies' Forgotten People*, 2nd ed. Melbourne University Press, Carlton, Victoria, 2007.

Bowen, Keith, *Geology of the Melbourne District*, Victoria, Geological Survey of Victoria, Mines Department, Bulletin No 59, Victorian Government Printer, Melbourne, 1967.

Bowler, James, *Port Phillip Survey 1957-1963. The Geology and Geomorphology, Memoirs of the National Museum of Victoria*, No.27, University of Melbourne, November 1966.

Braithwaite, Brian and Walsh, Noëll, *Things My Mother Should Have Told Me: The Best of Good Housekeeping 1922 – 1940*, Ebury Press, London, 1991.

Bunte, Jim, Hallman, Dave and Mueller, Heinz, *Vintage Toys: Robots and Space Toys*, Antique Trader Books, Iola, Wisconsin , USA, 1999.

Burnett, Frances *Little Lord Fauntleroy*,Scribners. New York, USA, 1886.

Butler, Graeme, & Associates, *Mornington Peninsula Shire Thematic History*, Attachment 5, Mornington Peninsula Shire, July 2013.

Calder,Winty, *Australian Aldershot: Langwarrin Military Reserve, Victoria, 1886 -1980*, Jimaringle Publications, Melbourne, 1987.

Cliff, Paul (ed.), *The Endless Playground: celebrating Australian childhood*, with introductory essays by Robert Holden and features by Jack Bedson…[et al.], National Library of Australia, Canberra, 2000.

Cockington, James, *Mondo Weirdo: Australia in the Sixties*, Mandarin, Port Melbourne, 1992.

Commonwealth Bureau of Census and Statistics, *2108.0 – Census of the Commonwealth of Australia, for 30th June 1954*, Vol II, Victoria, Part V, Commonwealth Government Printer, Canberra, September 1954.

Commonwealth Bureau of Census and Statistics, *2107.0 – Census of the Commonwealth of Australia, for 30th June 1961*, Vol II, Victoria, Part V, Commonwealth Government Printer, Canberra, August 1963.

Craven, Ian (ed.), with Martin Gray and Geraldine Stoneham, *Australian Popular Culture*, Cambridge University Press, Melbourne, 1994.

Davey, Gwenda and Seal, Graham, *A Guide to Australian Folklore: From Ned Kelly to Aeroplane Jelly*, Kangaroo Press, Roseville, New South Wales, 2003.

Davey, Philip, R., *When Hollywood Came to Melbourne: the story of the making of Stanley Kramer's On the beach*, Melbourne, 2005.

Delaney, Max et al. (eds.), *1956: Melbourne, Modernity and the XVI*

Olympiad, Museum of Modern Art at Heide, Bulleen, Victoria, 1996.

Education Department of Victoria, *Vision and Realisation : a centenary history of State Education in Victoria*, edited by Les Blake, Melbourne, 1973.

Frankston City Council, *Natural Reserves within Frankston City*, www.frankston.vic.gov.au, 2nd Edition, January 2010.

Frankston City Libraries, *Frankston Local History Pictures*, https://library.frankston.vic.gov. au.

Frankston Standard Leader newspaper, Issue 9 March 2009, Leader Associated Newspapers Pty Ltd, Mornington, Victoria, 2009.

Frankston Standard newspaper, E*astern Peninsula District School Sports in Pictures*, Issue 18 April, 1962, p.24, Standard Newspapers Limited, Frankston, Victoria.

History Teachers' Association of New South Wales, *Teaching History*, Vol 12, Part 2, Sydney, August 1978.

Howard, Dorothy, *Child's Play: Dorothy Howard and the Folklore of Australian Children*, edited by Kate Darian-Smith and June Factor, Museum Victoria, Melbourne, 2005.

Hutchinson, Woods, *A Handbook of Health*, 10th Ed., Houghton Mifflin Company, USA, 1911.

Jones, Michael, Frankston: *Resort to City,* Allen & Unwin, Sydney, 1989.

Kent, David, *Australian Chart Book 1940 -1969*, Australian Chart Book Pty Ltd, Turramurra, New South Wales, 2005.

Kent, Jacqueline, *In the Half Light: Life as a Child in Australia 1900 -1970*, Angus and Robertson, North Ryde, New South Wales, 1988.

Leach, Maria and Fried, Jerome (eds.), *Funk & Wagnalls Standard Dictionary of Folklore, Mythology and Legend*, one volume edition, Funk and Wagnalls, New York, 1972.

Lees, Stella, and Senyard, June, *The 1950s: How Australia Became a Modern Society, and Everyone Got a House and a Car*, Hyland House, South Yarra, Victoria, 1987.

Morrison, Dot , *Langwarrin Settlers and Soldiers*, Mornington Peninsula Family History Society Frankston, Victoria, 2008.

Murray, Mary, *A Home of My Own: Handy hints and images from domestic life in Australia in the 1940s and 1950s*, Mallon Publishing, Melbourne, 2001.

Nisbet, D. (ed.) and Cole, M., Langwarrin News, self-published, Langwarrin, Oct 1955 – Oct 1956.

O'Hanlon, S., 'Home Together, Home Apart: Boarding House, Hostel and Flat Life in Melbourne, c.1900-1940', PhD thesis, Monash University, 1999.

Parkin, Norma, Langwarrin, *100 years of Schooling 1890 – 1990*, 1st Ed, self-published, Australia, 1990.

Pascoe, Carla, *Spaces Imagined, Places Remembered: Childhood in 1950s Australia*, Cambridge Scholars Publishing, Newcastle upon Tyne, United Kingdom, 2011.

Peel, Lynette, *Rural Industry in the Port Phillip Region, 1835- 1880*, Melbourne University Press, Carlton, Victoria, 1974.

Public Record Office Victoria, Photographic Collection of Railway Negatives, www.prov.vic.gov.au.

Raworth, Bryce and Turnor, Martin, Frankston *Central Business District Heritage Review* (Report), Prepared for the City of Frankston, Bryce Raworth Pty. Ltd, Melbourne, 2010.

Rich, Mark, *100 Greatest Baby Boomer Toys*, Krause Publications, Iola, Wisconsin, USA, 2000.

Rowe, Susan, *Hastings Memories: a collection of reminiscences*, Hastings-Western Port Historical Society, 2007.

Scott, Ron, *The early history of Langwarrin*, Pax Printers & Publishers, Melbourne, 1966.

Shaw, A.G.L., *A history of the Port Phillip District : Victoria before separation*, Melbourne University Press, Carlton South, Victoria, 1996.

Short, Andrew, *Beaches of the Victorian Coast & Port Phillip Bay: A Guide to Their Nature, Characteristics, Surf and Safety*, Sydney University Press, Sydney, 1966.

State Library of Victoria Picture Collection, www.slv.vic.gov.au.

Thomas, Jordan, *The 1950s: Building a new Australia from the aftermath of war*, Trocadero Publishing, Sydney, 2011.

Townsend, Helen, *Baby Boomers: Growing up in Australia in the 1940s,50s and 60s*, Simon & Schuster, Brookvale, New South Wales, 1988.

Watkins, Kel, *Readin' 'ritin' 'rithmetic: Stories of School and School Days from 1898-1986 from the Coomandook and Coonalpyn Areas*, The Warrendi Project, Coomandook, South Australia, 1986.

Williams, Ron, *Born in 1956? What else happened?* Boom Books, Wickham, New South Wales, Australia, 2015.

Williams, Ron, *Born in 1955? What else happened?* Boom Books, Wickham, New South Wales, Australia, 2015.

Williams, Ron, *Born in 1950? What else happened?* Boom Books, Wickham, New South Wales, Australia, 2016.

About the Author

Savouring an orchard apple

Simon King is an emerging Australian author who has already published two books. *Crocodiles and Cocktails* (Hesperian Press, 2017) is based on the remote and pristine West Kimberley coastal region of Western Australia, where he spent a good part of his working life. *Witchcraft, whispers, shadows and strange sights* (Conscious Care Publishing, 2017), encompasses paranormal/supernatural encounters and events as well as matters dealing with associated folklore, myths and legends.

Simon's third book embraces his childhood being raised through the 1950s and early 1960s in a semi-rural area of Victoria when Australia was undergoing major economic and population growth following the Second World War. His experiences and memories are expressed reflecting on a bygone time and those long lost friends and special moments of that golden era in his life's journey.

Recent retirement from a long industrial career has provided him with the opportunity to compile his recollections and research many aspects of those times. Simon lives with his wife in Perth, Western Australia.

www.ingramcontent.com/pod-product-compliance
Lightning Source LLC
Chambersburg PA
CBHW071909290426
44110CB00013B/1338
9780648085447